Advance Praise for
Proclaim Liberty Throughout All the Land

"The United States is famous for its separation of church and state, but that has never meant separation of religion and politics. In *Proclaim Liberty Throughout All the Land*, Mark David Hall shows how Christianity has infused public life since the colonial era in profound and sometimes surprising ways. This book is not a case for 'Christian Nationalism.' But it makes a powerful case that America would look different—and worse—without the influence of Christian doctrines, communities, and believers."

—**Samuel Goldman**, Associate Professor, Department of Political Science, Executive Director, Loeb Institute for Religious Freedom, George Washington University

"Mark David Hall is one of our most outstanding scholars of early America, whose many distinguished publications have argued persuasively for the crucial importance of Christianity in the flourishing of America's experiment in ordered liberty. In *Proclaim Liberty Throughout All The Land*, he has placed at the disposal of readers the essential elements in the case he has made for Christianity's beneficial and indispensable influence. Never has a resource been more needed than this one is today."

—**Wilfred M. McClay**, Victor Davis Hanson Chair in Classical History and Western Civilization, and Professor of History, Hillsdale College

"The United States of America is a unique creation of freedom in the history of the world. That freedom is owed to its Judeo-Christian roots and philosophy. Mark David Hall has done an enormous service: Be the great scholar he is in answering the attacks on this great country's true foundation of freedom—faith—but communicate these facts, history, and responses in a way every American can read and understand. This is a great gift to our country, accessible to everyone."

—**Kelly Shackelford**, Esq., President, CEO, and Chief Counsel, First Liberty Institute

"This timely book is vital and indispensable for dispelling a popular, but disingenuous, narrative: that Christianity impeded equality and freedom in America. In his notably readable and reliable prose, Professor Hall with palpable civility and a rare command of history sets the record straight: Christianity in reality provided the motive, the predicate, and the catalyst for America's push for freedom and equality, including religious liberty for all in both society and in law."

—**Jeffery J. Ventrella**, Senior Counsel, SVP Academic Affairs & Training, Alliance Defending Freedom

PROCLAIM
LIBERTY
THROUGHOUT
ALL THE LAND

How Christianity Has
Advanced Freedom and Equality
for All Americans

MARK DAVID HALL

FIDELIS
BOOKS

A FIDELIS BOOKS BOOK
An Imprint of Post Hill Press
ISBN: 978-1-63758-723-2
ISBN (eBook): 978-1-63758-724-9

Cover Design by Conroy Accord

Interior Design by Yoni Limor

Post Hill Press
New York • Nashville
posthillpress.com

Published in the United States of America
1 2 3 4 5 6 7 8 9 10

This book is dedicated to the Alliance Defending Freedom, Becket, the Christian Legal Society, First Liberty Institute, and the Religious Freedom Institute. Their commitment to protecting the religious liberty of all citizens is worthy of our praise and support.

CONTENTS

INTRODUCTION

Christianity's role in American history is hotly contested in the academy and the public square. Scholars and popular authors regularly claim that Christianity—at least orthodox Christianity—has fostered oppression and intolerance. A common narrative is that liberty and equality have been advanced primarily when America's leaders embrace progressive manifestations of religion or reject faith altogether.

Andrew Seidel, for example, writes that Judeo-Christian principles are "thoroughly opposed to the principles upon which the United States was built."[1] Indeed, "Judeo-Christianity is not concerned with freedom or liberty—quite the opposite."[2] Matthew Stewart likewise contends that America's founders were successful because they rejected traditional Christianity and embraced a form of deism that was "functionally indistinguishable from what we would now call 'pantheism'; and pantheism is really just a pretty word for atheism.... America's founders were philosophical radicals."[3] Finally (and many more examples could be given) Mark Lilla argues that modern political advances became possible only when Enlightenment thinkers (including America's founders) rejected "the Christian tradition of thinking about politics" and embraced "a new approach to politics focused on human nature and human need."[4]

There is no question that Christianity has been used to justify evils such as slavery, poverty, sexism, and intolerance in America. However, such evils are not unique to the United States: they have existed, and exist, throughout the world in countries that embrace other religions and no religion. Yet it is also the case that Christians—motivated by their biblical and theological convictions—have done a great deal to right such wrongs. Scholars and writers, including authors who are not practicing Christians, have documented this reality with respect to world history. Rodney Stark's *The Victory of Reason: How Christianity Led to Freedom, Capitalism, and Western Success* and Tom Holland's *Dominion: How the Christian Revolution Remade the World* are two excellent places to start if you are interested in this global story.[5]

This book, *Proclaim Liberty Throughout All the Land*, focuses on the ways in which Christians have advanced liberty and equality in the American context. Contrary to many academics and popular authors, I show that Christians have regularly been motivated by their faith to create fair and just institutions, fight for political freedom, oppose slavery, and secure religious liberty for all. Of course, some Christians have appealed to the Bible and Christian theology to oppose such reforms or to justify evil practices. Americans of other faiths and no faith have also worked to advance liberty and equality for all. *Proclaim Liberty Throughout All the Land* cannot tell all of these stories; its more modest goal is to put to rest the myth that Christianity has been a regressive force with respect to positive political, legal, and societal reform in the United States.

Plan of the Book

In 2020, some Americans celebrated the four hundredth anniversary of the Pilgrims' landing in Plymouth, but many ignored this important event, or even lamented it.[6] This is vastly different from earlier anniversaries, where the Pilgrims and the Puritans who followed them were celebrated as apostles of freedom. For instance, in a speech commemorating the two hundredth anniversary of the Pilgrims' landing at Plymouth, the great orator and United States Senator Daniel Webster lauded these refugees as the authors of American "civil and religious liberty."[7]

In the mid-nineteenth century, it became popular to describe the Pilgrims and Puritans as dour, mean-spirted theocrats. For instance, Moses Coit Tyler, an important nineteenth-century literary critic, made the accusation that they "cultivated the grim and the ugly."[8] More recently, the journalist H. L. Mencken described them as harboring a "haunting fear that someone, somewhere, may be happy," and the playwright Arthur Miller explained that they were "theocrats" who desired to prevent "any kind of disunity."[9] In the first chapter, I respond to such critics. I acknowledge that Puritans were not twenty-first-century liberal democrats, but show that they respected the rule of law, created the most republican governments the world had ever seen, passed laws to protect women, children, and animals, and embraced a version of religious toleration.

The War for American Independence was, at its core, about liberty and equality. However, according to some critics, the patriots could not have been motivated by Christian ideas because the Bible prohibits rebellion and the war was unjust. Instead of Christianity, America's founders drew from other intellectual traditions to justify resisting British tyranny.[10]

In the second chapter, I show that American patriots drew from a long tradition of Jewish and Christian political thought that permits, and even requires, resistance to tyranny. Moreover, they had good reasons to believe that the Crown and Parliament planned to significantly infringe upon the colonists' constitutional and natural rights. The War for American Independence was a biblical and just war fought to secure political and religious liberty. It is no accident that one of the most prominent symbols of American freedom, the Liberty Bell, is inscribed with the biblical admonition to "proclaim liberty throughout all the land unto all inhabitants thereof."[11]

America's founders are routinely condemned because they owned slaves and did not immediately abolish this horrible institution. *The New York Times's 1619 Project* went so far as to assert that the War for American Independence was fought to preserve slavery and that the founders crafted a pro-slavery constitution.[12] *The 1619 Project* may be irresponsible, but numerous scholars, activists, and popular authors make similar, if less grossly inflated, claims. Furthermore, such charges are not just brought by secular authors. In a 2018 Fourth of July editorial, Mark Galli, editor of the influential magazine *Christianity Today*, asks, "Can we in any way, shape, or form say that America was founded on Christian principles when its very existence and prosperity were set on a foundation of unimaginable cruelty to millions of other human beings?" a question which he answers with a resounding "No!" The foundation of which he speaks is the oppression of African Americans and Native Americans.

In Chapter Three, I acknowledge that there is some truth to these accusations but argue that we should recognize that many founders never owned slaves, some

4

of those who did voluntarily freed them, and that many actively opposed the "peculiar institution." Indeed, slavery was voluntarily abolished or put on the road to extinction in eight states between 1776 and 1804, and significant steps were taken at the national level to end it. Unfortunately, the invention of the cotton gin in 1794 gave slavery a new lease on life in the American South.

There were relatively few evangelicals in eighteenth-century America, but their numbers exploded in the nineteenth century. The first priority for most evangelicals was sharing their faith, but a close second was reforming society. Among their chief concerns were the abolition of slavery and protecting the rights of Native Americans. Moreover, for the first time, numerous women—notably evangelical women—became involved in politics. Some historians attempt to explain this activism as an attempt to gain power or control others, but in the fourth chapter, I show that these nineteenth-century believers were motivated by their Christian convictions to seek freedom and justice for enslaved Africans and oppressed Native Americans.

Chapters Five, Six, and Seven shift directions by considering contemporary debates over religious liberty and church-state relations in the United States. Chapter Five departs from the major theme of this book by showing how nineteenth-century Protestants developed the idea that church and state must be strictly separated in order to deny liberty and equality to Roman Catholics. This anti-Catholic animus influenced twentieth-century Supreme Court justices, and it motivated the founders of organizations such as Protestants and Other Americans United for Separation of Church and State. It is necessary to understand this history if we are to appreciate how Christians came to work together to advance religious liberty for all after the Second World War.

Separationists are no longer motivated by anti-Catholicism; many are now driven by hatred of religion in general. Groups such as the Freedom From Religion Foundation, the American Humanist Association, and Americans United for Separation of Church and State regularly contend that religion must be stripped from the public square. So, for instance, they have argued that a cross from the First World War era on public land must be moved or destroyed, that Ohio should not be permitted to include a Star of David in its Holocaust Memorial, and that monuments of the Ten Commandments must be removed from public property. They have also used separationist rhetoric to argue against vouchers that would permit parents to send their children to faith-based schools, religious exemptions to general laws, and programs that rebuild churches, mosques, and synagogues in the wake of natural disasters. There are appropriate ways to separate church and state, but such separation need not limit the freedom of religious citizens and organizations or prevent them from being treated equally.

In Chapter Six, I contend that citizens must be free to express their religious convictions in the public square and that communities ought to be free to incorporate religious imagery and language into public building and monuments. I make historical and prudential arguments to support these positions. As well, I draw from personal experience serving as an expert witness in a case challenging the permissibility of a Ten Commandments monument on the State House grounds in Arkansas.

By the 1960s, almost all Americans agreed that religious freedom must be robustly protected. After the Supreme

Court made it more difficult to win religious liberty cases in *Employment Division v. Smith* (1990), Democrats and Republicans came together to enact the Religious Freedom Restoration Act of 1993. The act, which was intended to make it easier to win such cases, passed without a dissenting vote in the House, ninety-seven to three in the Senate, and was signed into law by President Bill Clinton.

Alas, this consensus began to collapse in the early twenty-first century. Academics started to publish books and articles with titles such as *Why Tolerate Religion?* and "What if Religion Is Not Special?"[13] In the political arena, the Obama Administration showed little concern for religious liberty when it required businesses to provide contraceptives and abortifacients to employees, even when owners had religious convictions against doing so. It also offered a rare challenge to the doctrine of ministerial exception, a legal protection requiring, in the words of Chief Justice John Roberts, that religious institutions must be free to decide "who will preach their beliefs, teach their faith, and carry out their mission."[14] The Trump Administration repaired some of this damage, but the Biden Administration has been less friendly to religious liberty than that of Obama's.

Chapter Seven explains why this shift occurred and offers multiple reasons for robustly protecting the religious liberty of all citizens. I make arguments based on the historic understanding of the Free Exercise Clause but also offer principled and prudential reasons as to why we should robustly protect what many founders called "the sacred right of conscience." I also show that Christian legal organizations have been among the best advocates for religious liberty for all, including citizens who embrace non-Christian faiths.

In the concluding chapter, I suggest that *Proclaim Liberty Throughout All the Land* could have been much longer by briefly pointing out additional ways Christians have advanced liberty and equality throughout American history. I acknowledge again that Christians have sometimes resisted these advances and that members of other faiths, and no faith, have advocated for these ends. At the same time, there should be no doubt that it is simply false to claim that that liberty and equality have been advanced primarily when America's leaders embrace progressive manifestations of religion or reject faith altogether.

CHAPTER ONE

The Puritans Were NOT
Tyrannical Theocrats

The Stereotype

In a speech commemorating the two hundredth anniversary of the Pilgrims' landing at Plymouth, the great orator Daniel Webster lauded these refugees as the authors of American "civil and religious liberty."[15] A few decades later, Alexis de Tocqueville observed that "Puritanism was not only a religious doctrine, but also at several points it was mingled with the most absolute democratic and republican theories." He contended that understanding this "point of departure" is "the key to the whole book"—his magisterial *Democracy in America*.[16]

In 2020, some Americans celebrated the four hundredth anniversary of the Pilgrims' landing in Plymouth, many ignored it, and some even lamented it.[17] These naysayers accept the all-too-common views that the Pilgrims were dour Christians who, according to Nathaniel Hawthorne, wore "sad-colored garments" or, in the words of the nineteenth-century English professor Moses Coit Tyler, "cultivated the grim and the ugly."[18]

More recently, the journalist H. L. Mencken described them as harboring a "haunting fear that someone, somewhere, may be happy," and the playwright Arthur Miller explained that they were "theocrats" who desired to prevent "any kind of disunity."[19] Contemporary authors such as Steven Waldman, who often writes well on the subject of religion in America, characterizes them as "sadistic" authoritarians.[20]

The Pilgrims, and the Puritans who followed them, were not twenty-first-century liberal democrats, but they created political institutions and practices that profoundly influenced the course of American politics and facilitated later experiments in republican self-government and liberty under law. They valued natural rights, government by the consent of the governed, and limited government; they were convinced that citizens have a right, and perhaps even a duty, to resist tyrannical governments.

Very Brief History

To understand the Puritans, we must briefly consider the Protestant Reformation. This movement may be conveniently dated to 1517, when Martin Luther (1483–1546) nailed his Ninety-Five Theses to the Wittenberg castle church door. For the purposes of this and the following chapter, I will focus on the Calvinist (or Reformed) wing of the Reformation. This is because the Pilgrims and Puritans were Calvinists, and ideas developed within the Reformed tradition of political reflection had a tremendous influence in early New England and, later, on many patriots in the War of American Independence.

Although John Calvin (1509–1564) was born in France, he lived most of his adult life in Geneva, Switzerland, which he helped govern between 1536 and 1538 and then between 1541 and 1564. In 1536, he published the first edition of his *Institutes of the Christian Religion*, a volume that he revised several times until its final 1559 edition.[21] Calvin's works echo the great battle cries of the Reformation such as *sola gratia, sola fide*, and *sola scriptura*; and it reinforced the seminal notion of the priesthood of all believers. Reformers rejected the ideas that the church and its priests were necessary intermediaries between common persons and God, and that the church as an institution possessed the authority to speak for Him. Individuals were told that they were responsible for their relationship with God, and that His will for them is most clearly revealed in the Holy Scriptures. These last two beliefs led to a heavy emphasis on literacy and a commitment to translating and printing the Bible in the vernacular (i.e., the common language, as opposed to Latin). Without widespread literacy, how could everyone read and interpret the Bible for themselves?[22]

The impact of the explosion of literacy in Protestant countries cannot be overestimated. As one scholar of literacy put it: "Protestants tended to be more literate than Catholics within areas where they co-existed, and countries where the Reformed faith was the official religion were usually more advanced in literacy than Catholic neighbours."[23] In the mid-seventeenth century, literacy rates of Roman Catholic Italy and France were 23 percent and 29 percent.[24] By way of contrast, around 95 percent of seventeenth-century males in New England were literate.[25] Widespread literacy helped undermine existing hierarchies and paved the way for the growth of republican self-government.

Harvard College

In 1636, the Puritans founded Harvard College. The most important reason for doing so was to produce an educated clergy, but as Samuel Eliot Morison points out, "the purpose of the founders was much broader than that; and the curriculum they established was not a divinity curriculum."[26] According to the college's first charter (1650), its goal was the "advancement of all good literature, arts and science."[27] Five years earlier, its president had requested funds to purchase books on "law, physics, philosophy, and mathematics" that would be "both honorable and profitable to the country in general and in special to the scholars."[28] Harvard was a deeply Christian institution, and about half of its graduates in this era did indeed go on to be ministers.[29] Its motto was *Veritas* (Truth), and *In Christi Gloriam* (for the glory of Christ) "was inscribed on the first college seal, and the college laws enjoined all students to 'lay Christ in the bottom, as the only foundation of knowledge and learning.'"[30]

The Reformation had several false starts in England, most notably those led by John Wycliffe (1320–1384) and William Tyndale (1494–1536); both famous for translating the Bible into English (a crime for which Tyndale was burned at the stake). England's King Henry VIII was not particularly interested in Protestantism, but he did want to divorce his wife, Catherine of Aragon, and marry Anne Boleyn. Because the pope refused to annul his marriage to Catherine, he cut ties with Rome in 1534 and created the Church of England. Henry made himself rather than the pope the head of this new church, but otherwise, he was largely content to leave it alone.

Henry's daughter Mary was a serious Catholic, and after she became Queen in 1553, she persecuted and killed Protestant leaders, actions that earned her the pejorative nickname "Bloody Mary." Many English Protestant leaders fled England for Calvin's Geneva. After Mary died in 1558, these "Marian exiles" returned to England with a renewed desire to "purify" the Church of England. In 1564, they were first called "Puritans" by their opponents.

Most English Puritans were content *merely* to purify the Church of England, but a subset of them saw no biblical precedent for a national church. They thought that each Christian congregation should govern itself. Because of their desire to separate from any sort of national church, they became known as "Separatists."[31] In order to freely practice their faith, a group of them fled to Holland in 1608 and then to America aboard the Mayflower in 1620.

Before these English Separatists (more commonly known as Pilgrims) disembarked from the *Mayflower*, they made an agreement that represents an important political innovation. This covenant, known today as the Mayflower Compact, committed the people and the rulers to "the Glory of God, and the Advancement of the Christian Faith, and the Honour of our King and Country." Its legitimacy stemmed from the consent of the forty-one men—most, but not all, of whom were Separatists—who signed the document.[32]

Some scholars have attempted to downplay the importance of the Mayflower Compact, pointing out (accurately) that it was not well known until the nineteenth century and was not even called the "Mayflower Compact" until 1793.[33] These facts are true but irrelevant. The Compact is important because it represents the commitment many Reformed thinkers had to the idea that people must consent to civic and ecclesiastical institutions if they are to be legitimate. The Pilgrims and the Puritans who followed them created civil governments that were among the most republican the world had ever seen.[34]

Prior to the Protestant Reformation, most Christian thinkers contended that either a monarchy, or a monarchy checked by a legislative body, was the ideal form of government. The Protestant emphasis on literacy, the priesthood of all believers, and, in many cases, congregational forms of government, helped to undercut hierarchical forms of government (both ecclesiastical and civil). In the seventeenth century, Protestant Reformers began to argue for the first time that the Bible *only* sanctioned republican governments. They adopted this idea from what might seem at first to be an unlikely source: commentaries on the Old Testament written by Jewish rabbis.

Reformers believed that ministers and scholars should read the Bible in its original languages. This led many of them to learn Hebrew. More significantly for our purposes, as Eric Nelson explains in his wonderful book *The Hebrew Republic*, "to understand the Hebrew Bible, they insisted, one should consult the full array of rabbinic sources that were now available to the Christian West. One should turn to the Talmud and midrash, to the targums and medieval law codes."[35] In these texts, Protestant Reformers discovered a set of ideas that scholars now refer to as "political Hebraism."

The most important political idea Reformed thinkers drew from rabbinical commentaries was that republics were the *only* form of government approved by the Bible. From these commentaries, they learned to interpret passages such as I Samuel 8 as condemning the Jewish people because they desired a *king*, not because they desired a ruler other than God.[36] By the mid-seventeenth century, most Reformed leaders had come to embrace these views in theory, and civic leaders in Puritan New England had the ability to put these ideas into action as early as 1620.[37]

The Mayflower Compact is a great example of Hebraic republicanism, but it is far from unique. In the 1630s, great waves of non-Separatist Puritans came to New England where they created literally hundreds of ecclesiastical and civil covenants whereby people joined together before the eyes of God to pursue specific ends ultimately aimed at glorifying God.[38] Each of these covenants reinforced the idea that governments are legitimate and binding because they were established by the consent of the governed. This view is reflected well by Henry Wolcott's notes of a 1638 election sermon by one of Connecticut's founders, Thomas Hooker:

> Doctrine. I. That the choice of public magistrates belongs unto the people by God's own allowance.
>
> II. The privilege of election, which belongs to the people, therefore must not be exercised according to their humors, but according to the blessed will and law of God.

III. They who have the power to appoint officers and magistrates, it is in their power also to set the bounds and limitations of power and place unto which they call them.

Reasons. I. Because the foundation of authority is laid, firstly, in the free consent of the people.[39]

Not only did the people consent to the formation of a government, but most men could also participate in town meetings and freemen could be elected representatives of the General Court. Of course, there was an expectation that citizens would elect and defer to godly, talented magistrates, a point John Winthrop famously lectured Massachusetts Bay's General Court about in 1645.[40] Puritans were not twenty-first-century liberal democrats, but the political institutions they created and promulgated contributed to the way Americans thought about politics. These political commitments help explain why the colonies reacted so forcefully to perceived acts of British tyranny in the 1760s and 1770s, and why the constitutions they created as independent states were even more democratic than the ones they had inherited from Britain. But that is getting ahead of the story.

The Puritans as Theocrats?

Early Puritan colonies are often described as theocracies, but this cannot be the case if by "theocracy" we mean either rule directly by God or rule by priests.[41] As we have seen, the Puritans adopted remarkably democratic forms of government. Non-Separatists were permitted to consent to the Mayflower Compact and were included in Plymouth Colony's civic life. Clergy in Massachusetts Bay were initially banned from holding civic offices, and early Puritan legal codes specifically prohibited European institutions such as ecclesiastical courts. As well, these statutes stipulated that ecclesiastical sanctions such as excommunication had no impact on civic office holders.[42]

This is not to say that elected officials had no role in protecting and promoting Christianity. From the time of Constantine, almost every Christian author who addressed the subject believed rulers should do so. Indeed, David D. Hall observes:

> On both sides of the Protestant-Catholic divide, theologians and civic leaders agreed that true religion could be readily defined...[and] God empowered godly kings or, as was also said, the "Christian prince," to use the powers of the civil state in behalf of true religion.[43]

The question was not whether rulers should support true religion, but how they should do so. The Puritans indisputably desired to create Christian social and political institutions that they believed were faithful to the Holy Scriptures. This mission is illustrated well by the 1672 declaration by the Connecticut General Court: "We have endeavoured not only to ground our capital laws upon the Word of God, but also all other laws upon the justice and equity held forth in that Word, which is a most perfect rule."[44] However, the implications of this approach are far from theocratic, at least as the term is usually used.

The influence of Scripture upon New England's laws is most obvious in each colony's capital laws. Crimes such as adultery and incest were not punished by death in England, but the Puritans, looking to the Old Testament for guidance, made them capital offenses. Lest there be any mistake about the biblical warrant for this punishment, each capital law cited scriptural authority. For instance,

> If any child, or children, above sixteen years old, and of sufficient under-standing, shall curse, or smite their natural father, or mother; he or they shall be put to death: unless it can be sufficiently testified that the Parents have been very unchristianly negligent in the education of such children; or so provoked them by extreme, and cruel correction: that they have been forced thereunto to preserve themselves from death or maiming. Exod. 21. 17. Lev. 20. 9. Exod. 21. 15.[45]

Such laws are harsh, but in practice, the death penalty was rarely enforced. Only three people were hanged for adultery in Puritan New England, and no one was ever put to death for being disrespectful to his/her parents.[46]

On balance, the Puritans' use of Scripture as a guide for criminal law had a liberalizing effect. In seventeenth-century England, a person could be put to death based on circumstantial evidence, but the Puritans, drawing from Deuteronomy 19:15 ("One witness shall not rise up against a man for any iniquity, or for any sin, in any sin that he sinneth: at the mouth of two witnesses..."), required two witnesses to the same act in capital cases.[47] Similarly, a third of all English criminals were sentenced to death; a person could be executed for stealing property worth little more than a shilling. But American Puritans interpreted biblical texts such as Exodus 22:4 ("If the theft is certainly found alive in his hand, whether it is an ox or donkey or sheep, he shall restore double") to require restitution as the penalty for theft rather than death.[48]

The Puritan legal revisions were extensive. David D. Hall observes in his magisterial *The Puritans* that they included "[adding] a cluster of rights and privileges for plaintiffs and defendants.... Out went torture, high fees, and long delays.... Overnight, the cruelties of the English law and the abuses of power and money it sanctioned gave way to the value of peace, 'mutual love,' and equity."[49] American law owes much to these biblically inspired Puritans.

Nursing Fathers

The Puritans considered civil magistrates to be "nursing fathers" (a phrase taken from Isaiah 49:23) to the church, and so like most countries and colonies, they established churches. The only European colony or country that declined to have an established church in this era—Rhode Island (also known as "Rogues' Island")—was viewed by almost everyone as an experiment gone horribly wrong. It was commonplace to require church attendance, support the favored church with tax revenue, give special privileges to its ministers, and place restrictions on dissenters.[50] Yet the Puritans rejected European practices such as ecclesiastical courts, and they made church membership voluntary.[51] It would be inaccurate to say they embraced religious liberty, but neither did they have an "Inquisition or a central group of clergy who enforced conformity."[52]

In the late seventeenth century, Pennsylvania and a few other colonies declined to create official established churches, and, unlike Rhode Island, they were viewed as being reasonably successful.[53] However, even in these colonies there were religious tests for civic offices, and the government actively punished vice and promoted religion. For instance, Article 37 of Pennsylvania's first laws (1682) held that magistrates should punish

> such offences against God, as swearing, cursing, lying, profane talking, drunkenness, drinking of healths, obscene words, incest, sodomy, rapes, whoredom, fornication, and other uncleanness (not to be repeated)...all prizes, stage-plays, cards, dice, May-games, gamesters, masques, revels, bull-battings, cock-fighting, bear-battings, and the like, which excite the people to rudeness, cruelty, looseness, and irreligion.[54]

My point here is *not* that religious tests are a good thing or that governments should punish "vices" such as playing with cards and dice; it is that the Puritans were absolutely *not* unusual in embracing such policies. Yet some Puritan moral legislation was ahead of its time, such as the prohibition of "tyranny or cruelty towards any brute creatures which are usually kept for the use of man."[55]

Puritans were more tolerant than is often assumed. For instance, Protestant dissenters, i.e., non-Congregationalists, were tolerated if they remained quiet and did not disturb the public order. Massachusetts law recognized that civic authorities should not attempt to "constrain [citizens] to believe or profess against their consciences."[56] In other words, Puritan rulers did not attempt to compel belief. This is a *type* of religious toleration, and it is one that literally billions of people living in countries such as China, Burma, Saudi Arabia, and North Korea wish they had today.

As in every other country populated by Christians in the seventeenth century, religious dissenters were at best tolerated, if they were not discriminated against, persecuted, or banned.[57] And heresy was regularly punishable by law. In a few places, such as the colony of New Haven, people were punished because of their beliefs, but most Puritans—certainly those in Massachusetts Bay—were more concerned that heretics "tending to the subversion of the Christian faith, and destruction of the souls of men, ought duly to be restrained."[58] Similarly, Anabaptists were banned from the colony, not because they held erroneous views but because in the past "they have been the incendiaries of commonwealths" and "troublers of churches."[59] Troublesome dissenters such as Roger Williams (1636) and Anne Hutchinson (1638) were given multiple chances to repent, but when they continued to disturb the peace—at least in the minds of local civic leaders—they were banished from the colony.

Simply put, the Puritans were not "theocrats" as the term is usually defined. Moreover, they embraced a form of religious toleration, and few if any colonies or countries were ahead of them in this regard. There was much room for improvement, and fortunately, their Christian political ideas contained seeds that would grow into a constitutional principle that offered substantial protection of the "free exercise of religion."

Limited Government and Bills of Rights

The Puritan conviction that rulers should promote true religion and virtue suggests a powerful state, but this possibility was tempered by their view that civil power must be strictly limited. Puritans believed that all humans are sinful and that even Christians continue to struggle with sin (Romans 7: 13–25). Like Lord Acton, they understood that "power tends to corrupt, and absolute power corrupts absolutely."[60] Accordingly, they placed a variety of checks on rulers, including regular elections and legal restraints on civic officials.

Among the most significant innovations was the 1641 Massachusetts Body of Liberties. These statutes contained many protections later found in the Bill of Rights, including protections against governments taking private property without just compensation and prohibitions against double jeopardy, torture, and "in-humane Barbarous or cruel" bodily punishments. Seven years later, these laws were revised and published as *The Book of the General Lawes Liberties and Liberties Concerning the Inhabitants of Massachusetts*. This was the first printed code of laws in the Western world, an innovation that made it possible to distribute the laws more widely than if they were copied by hand.[61] In Michael Winship's words, in "New England, the colonists created [legal] systems that were simple, equitable, inexpensive, speedy, transparent, and grounded in law codes crafted to protect colonists' rights against overbearing local rulers."[62]

The Puritans also believed the power of the state was constrained by what the minister John Davenport called in 1670 the "Law of Nature," which is "God's law."[63] A striking expression of this idea is found in a 1678 sermon by Massachusetts's Samuel Nowell entitled "Abraham in Arms," where he contended that the "Law of nature... teaches men self-preservation." He proceeded to point out that there "is such a thing as Liberty and Property given to us, both by the Laws of God & Men, when these are invaded, we may defend ourselves."[64]

Nowell preached the sermon shortly after King Philips War (1675–1678), but his comment that God "has set rulers their bounds and by his law hath determined people's liberties and property" suggests that active resistance to rulers who violate a people's rights is justifiable.[65] When Reformed Americans in the late eighteenth century made natural law and natural rights arguments against abuses of the Crown, they were drawing in large part from their own tradition, one that may be traced back to the early days of the Reformation as well as earlier Christian thinkers.[66]

Like their descendants, Puritans were concerned with "liberty," but it is critical to recognize that they never understood the concept to include the more recent idea that men and women should be free to do anything except physically harm others. They distinguished between liberty and personal license. Puritans were primarily interested with freedom from sin, but they also viewed liberty as the ability of a people to govern themselves and to do what God requires of them. The closest they came to embracing modern notions of liberty was with respect to freedom of conscience, but as we have seen, religiously motivated *actions* judged to be disruptive by the community could still be restricted. As Barry Alan Shain has demonstrated, this constrained understanding of liberty remained dominant in America until well into the twentieth century.[67]

But Did They Have Fun?

Nathaniel Hawthorne's story "The May-Pole of Merry Mount" describes the whimsical residents of Merry Mount as feasting and dancing around a Maypole. Merry Mount, a town near Plymouth, was led by Thomas Morton, "Lord of Misrule." In Hawthorne's account, their celebration is interrupted by "dismal" Puritans led by Myles Standish who disapprove of such "jollity." Accordingly, the Puritans cut down the Maypole and arrested Morton. Such stories likely informed the journalist H.L. Mencken's definition of Puritanism as "the haunting fear that someone, somewhere, may be happy."[68]

"The May-Pole of Merry Mount"

The real Thomas Morton failed in several ventures before joining forces with two "erstwhile pirates," Humphrey Rastall and Richard Wollaston, to form an outpost in New England to compete with Plymouth in the fur trade.[69] After Rastall and Wollaston returned to

England, Morton organized a mutiny and renamed the outpost "Ma-re Mount." William Bradford's account of the controversy reveals that the Pilgrims were troubled by the drunkenness and fornication associated with the outpost, but most concerning of all was their belief that Morton was selling guns and ammunition to Native Americans. Myles Standish did indeed lead a force to arrest Morton and his men, who were "'so steeled with drink' that they could not lift their weapons."[70] Morton was arrested and returned to England, but, according to John Taylor, if there was a Maypole, "the Pilgrims left it standing."[71] The Pilgrims opposed Morton for spiritual, moral, and economic reasons, but their primary concern was that he was engaged in trade that could lead to Plymouth's destruction. However one weighs these motives, it is evident that they were not simply opposed to merriment.

The English Puritans garnered a reputation of being killjoys almost immediately because, after coming into power in England, they prohibited a wide range of activities on Sunday, including commerce, games, travel, dancing, secular songs, and drunkenness. They also banned theaters (1641), maypoles (1644), and Christmas (1645).[72] American Puritans continued many of these prohibitions because they associated these holidays or practices with the Roman Catholic Church and/or thought them to be unbiblical. But they did not have an abstract objection to having a good time.

According to one of the greatest students of the Puritans, Edmund Morgan:

the Puritan was no ascetic...he never praised hair shirts or dry crusts. He liked good food, good drink, and homely comforts; and while he laughed at mosquitos, he found it a real hardship to drink water when the beer ran out. In using the good things of this world, however, he kept in mind the order which God had ordained; he sought God's glory in "eating and drinking, sleeping and recreating."[73]

A "hardship to drink water"? Indeed. It was not uncommon for men to drink beer for breakfast, lunch, and dinner. One of the most prized student jobs at Harvard was "that of butler; for he kept the keys to the buttery and dispensed the beer for breakfast, dinner, and supper."[74] It is not difficult to imagine that the butler, upon occasion, served extra rations of beer to his friends after supper. In the words of a recent historian, the Puritans "positively loved beer."[75]

The Puritans banned feasts associated with Roman Catholicism, and in *The Scarlet Letter*, Nathaniel Hawthorne suggests that they "compressed whatever mirth and public joy they deemed allowable to human infirmity" to the single day when the new governor takes office.[76] Hawthorne was correct that these "election days" were quite festive, but he is wrong to suggest no other days were. David D. Hall reports that "[f]easting, dancing, drinking—these were how the people of New England celebrated weddings as a rite of passage.... Funerals involved food and drink, as did every ordination of a minister."[77] Militia training days regularly ended with men retiring to a tavern.[78]

In *The Scarlet Letter*, Nathaniel Hawthorne described Puritans as wearing "sad-colored garments," and the nineteenth-century English professor Moses Coit Tyler observed that Puritans "cultivated the grim and the ugly." [79] These images persist in the popular imagination. In reality, the Pilgrims "clearly had a taste for a wide range of bright colors. Historians who have investigated estate inventories in Plymouth Colony have uncovered countless references to red, blue, green, yellow, and russet (orange-brown) garments."[80] And although the Puritans objected to musical instruments and art in churches because they did not see biblical warrant for them, they had no principled objection to art, and they entertained themselves by playing music.[81]

When it came to sex, the Puritans rejected the "popish conceit of the excellence of virginity."[82] They did not believe that it was more holy to abstain from sex; indeed, they viewed sex within the bounds of marriage to be a positive good. John Cotton wrote that

> Women are creatures without which there is no comfortable living for man: it is true of them what is wont to be said of governments, *that bad ones are better than none*: They are a sort of blasphemers then who despise and decry them, and call them *a necessary evil*, for they are *a necessary good* (emphasis in original).[83]

Ministers criticized both husbands and wives who denied their spouse the pleasures of the wedding bed, and doing so could result in church discipline. James Mattock, for instance, was expelled from First Church of Boston for denying conjugal fellowship to his wife.[84]

What About Mary Dyer and the Salem Witch Trials?

Those who characterize the Puritans as intolerant theocrats often highlight two events: the hanging of the Quaker Mary Dyer on Boston Commons and the Salem witchcraft trials. These acts were unjust and must be condemned, but they should not define the Puritans. A little historical context helps us to better understand these incidents.

Massachusetts Bay, like other colonies, banned disruptive and dangerous sects, including Jesuits, Anabaptists, and Quakers. Quakers are not Anabaptists, but the Puritans often conflated the two. This is important, because never far from the minds of civic rulers was the 1534–1535 Munster rebellion in Germany. Believing they were acting on God's direct commands, Anabaptists took over the city, instituted plural marriages, redistributed property, and eventually started executing dissenters. The rebellion ended in a bloodbath. Colonial authorities regularly referenced the events of Munster when explaining why it was necessary to ban Anabaptists and Quakers. For instance, the General Court of Massachusetts referenced Munster shortly after they hanged two Quakers on Boston Common in 1659 (discussed below).[85]

The Society of Friends was founded in England around 1652. Its members are referred to as "Friends" or "Quakers," the latter nickname perhaps coming from their proclivity to become so excited in worship services that they would literally quake. There is no question that early Friends could be very disruptive. Perhaps most famously, the Quaker leader John Naylor rode into Bristol, England on Palm Sunday 1656, allowing "his flatters to strew garments in his way as they sang 'Holy, holy, holy, Lord God of Israel.'"[86] Tried before Parliament, he barely escaped the death penalty but was sentenced to be flogged and branded with a "B" for blasphemer.

In 1657, three Quakers, William Robinson, Marmaduke Stevenson, and Mary Dyer, arrived in Boston. Viewed as disruptive heretics, they were imprisoned and then banished upon pain of death. Robinson and Stevenson refused to leave and were kept in prison, whereas Dyer left but later returned. In 1659, the three Quakers were banished a second time, and again the men refused to leave. Dyer departed and, once again, returned. At this point, all three were sentenced to death. The two men were hanged, but Dyer was granted a last-minute reprieve and was banished once more. She left Boston and, probably to no one's surprise, later returned. This time, she was hanged. A fourth Quaker was executed in 1661. Four Quakers hanged on Boston Common are four too many, but it should be noted that they were banished not for their beliefs per se but because they were viewed as being disruptive and dangerous to the social order. All four were executed for violating the terms of their banishment.[87]

From 1656 to 1661, approximately forty Quakers were imprisoned, whipped, and banished from New England colonies, and four were executed.[88] By way of contrast, in England, more than 10,000 Friends were imprisoned, and 242 died because of abuse, mistreatment, or neglect.[89] In 1661, King Charles II ordered the Massachusetts General

Court to stop maiming and killing Quakers. The Court "complied, but only as a gesture of respect to Charles, it insisted, not because it had to obey his orders."[90] More significantly, after 1660, the movement became far less disruptive and began to emphasize its commitment to pacifism and quietism.[91] These changes contributed a great deal to the eventual acceptance of Quakers throughout the British Empire.

In 1692, another threat to Winthrop's "City on a Hill" arose, this time in Salem, Massachusetts. When all was said and done, fourteen women and six men were convicted of witchcraft and executed (nineteen were hanged and one was pressed to death when being interrogated). These were not the only executions for witchcraft in New England, but prior to Salem, they had become quite rare. In the twenty-nine years preceding the Salem witch trials, there had only been one execution for witchcraft in the entire region. In part, this was because ministers and civic officials had put stringent procedures in place to protect men and women accused of witchcraft; protections that were ignored at the Salem trials.[92]

It may strike modern readers as utterly ridiculous to try and punish witches, but this is only because most people no longer believe in them. C. S. Lewis observed in *Mere Christianity* that

> Three hundred years ago people in England were putting witches to death... but surely the reason we do not execute witches [today] is that we do not believe there are such things. If we did—if we

> really thought that there were people
> going about who had sold themselves
> to the devil and received supernatural
> powers from him in return and were
> using these powers to kill their neigh-
> bors or drive them mad or bring bad
> weather, surely we would all agree that
> if anyone deserved the death penalty,
> then these filthy quislings did?[93]

Belief in witchcraft was common in the seventeenth century, and as Lewis suggests, witchcraft trials were not limited to Massachusetts Bay. Even Rhode Island, which did not require the death penalty for any offense against the First Table of the Law (those commandments prohibiting offenses against God such as idolatry and blasphemy), considered witchcraft to be a violent crime against others and so made it a capital offense.

Between 1400 and 1775, 100,000 men and women in the European world were prosecuted as witches. Of these, 50,000 were sentenced to death.[94] By way of contrast, 272 Americans were formally charged with witchcraft and 32 were executed.[95] State-sanctioned executions for witch-craft in Europe continued well into the eighteenth century, the last ones occurring in 1718 (France), 1722 (Scotland), and 1782 (Switzerland). The last execution for witchcraft in England was in 1683; in America, it occurred in 1692 as a result of the trials in Salem. After these trials, Massachu-setts never tried another person for witchcraft.[96]

The Salem witchcraft trials occurred under the authority of the Royal Governor Sir William Phips. As Michael Winship points out, Phips "had no formal education and perhaps could not even read, let alone write. Far from being an experienced saint and Congregationalist, Phips had only been baptized and joined Boston's Second Church in 1690"; he was "Massachusetts's first post-puritan governor."[97] Phips created a special court presided over by William Stroughton, the crown-appointed deputy governor. Stroughton promptly threw out legal protections which had previously resulted in a 25 percent conviction rate for accused witches. In his hands, the rates rose to 100 percent.[98]

Particularly problematic for the Salem trials was the reliance on "spectral" evidence—that is, reports by witnesses claiming to see the "specter" (spirit) of an accused person outside of his or her body. New England ministers had long warned against the use of such unreliable evidence, but under Phips and Stroughton, it played a key role in convicting the accused. The trials indisputably whipped the local population—including ministers—into a frenzy, but in the final analysis, the trials, rather than being quintessentially Puritan, were—in the words of Michael Winship—a "horrific fluke."[99]

By placing the hanging of Quakers and the Salem witch trials in their historical context, I am in no way condoning them. My argument is simply that the Puritans were not that different from many other people in the era, and they were more humane than many. As such, it is inappropriate to focus on these events to the exclusion of the Puritans' many accomplishments—accomplishments that paved the way for American independence and the creation of a constitutional order that has done a great deal of good.

Conclusion

The Puritans were not twenty-first century democrats, but neither were they intolerant theocrats. They created political institutions that were more democratic than any the world had ever seen, and they strictly limited civic leaders by law. They valued liberty—properly understood—and in fact had, in the words of David D. Hall, an "animus against 'tyranny' and 'arbitrary' power that pervaded virtually every sermon and political statement."[100] This sentiment became particularly relevant in 1764 when, from the Patriot perspective, the British government embarked on a long train of abuses designed to destroy American liberty.

CHAPTER TWO

The War for American Independence

The War for American Independence was fundamentally about liberty and equality. Yet according to some critics, the patriots could not have been motivated by Christian ideas because the Bible prohibits rebellion and the conflict violates the Christian just war tradition. Instead of Christianity, America's founders drew from other intellectual traditions, such as a secularized Lockean liberalism, to justify resisting British tyranny.

Mark A. Noll, Nathan O. Hatch, and George M. Marsden—three of the most prominent students of religion in American history—propose a version of this argument in their influential book *The Search for Christian America*.[101] Historians often have a hard time making moral judgements about the past, and Noll, Hatch, and Marsden are no exception. Technically, they conclude "it is difficult to see how Christians can without qualification defend the innate justice of the war."[102] This conclusion is vague, and it reveals a fundamental misunderstanding of the just war tradition which presupposes that no war can ever be perfectly "just." Such a state of affairs is not part of temporal realities. Rather, the tradition assumes *relative* justice as an ideal in the affairs of human beings and nations and consequently seeks moral wisdom and discernment in arriving at judgments about war and peace.[103] The War for American Independence was not "innately just" or just "without qualification"; no war ever has been or could be—not even America's most obviously just war, the Second World War. The question is whether the War of American Independence was *justified*. Strictly speaking, Noll, Hatch, and Marsden leave open the possibility that it was, but the overall tenor of their work makes it evident that they think it was not.[104]

Gregg Frazer of the Master's College is a political scientist, not a historian, and does not hesitate to make moral judgements. In an essay entitled "The American Revolution: Not a Just War," he argues that the patriots were manipulative propagandists complaining about "slight taxes" and whose constitutional arguments were clearly in error, as "the British Constitution did not require that those taxed be represented at all."[105] He recognizes that many Americans were Calvinists, but thinks it absurd that they would appeal to Calvin because this Magisterial Reformer "made it abundantly clear that rebellion was never justified."[106] Similarly, Andrew Seidel asserts that the "Declaration of Independence is an anti-Christian document" because in Romans 13, "Paul claims that governments are instituted for men by God and that rebellion against the government is rebellion against God."[107]

In addition to their actions being unbiblical, Frazer calculates that the patriots violated four separate just war "guidelines" and concludes that the "American Revolution...was by the standards of 'just war' theory, not a just war."[108] The ethicist John Keown outdoes Frazer by concluding that "it is far from obvious" that the War for American Independence" satisfies *any* of the seven criteria that he believes must be meet if a war is to be considered just. Remarkably, he even suggests that the American victory may have been "a cause of the blood-bath that was the French Revolution."[109]

Romans 13, Tyranny, and the Reformed Tradition

Whether the War for American Independence was biblical seems, at first glance, to be a question of interest only to Christians who view the Bible as the inspired word of God, but it is one that should matter to anyone who is curious about which intellectual traditions influenced America's founders. If the Bible prohibits rebellion against tyrannical rulers, either the patriots didn't care what the Bible says, or they were more influenced by intellectual traditions that permit revolution. Although Americans did, in fact, draw from a variety of intellectual traditions when they broke from Great Britain, there was no question in their minds that the Bible permitted rebellion against tyrants.

On the surface, biblical passages like Romans 13:1–2 seem to leave little room for Christians to actively resist tyrannical rulers:

> Let every soul be subject unto the higher powers. For there is no power but of God: the powers that be are ordained by God. Whosoever therefore resists the power, resists the ordinance of God: and they that resist shall receive to themselves damnation.

With notable exceptions, prior to the Protestant Reformation, Christian thinkers taught that the Bible prohibited armed resistance to tyrannical governments.[110] If a ruler ordered citizens to disobey God, they should refuse to obey—and take the consequences. Passive resistance was generally permitted, but active resistance, especially armed resistance against a tyrannical ruler, was strictly prohibited. Martin Luther (1483–1546), John Calvin (1509–1564), and other early Reformers initially embraced this view, but they quickly changed their minds. Because Calvinism was a dominant religious influence on America's founders, I focus on how thinkers in this tradition have addressed the question of resisting tyrannical rulers.[111]

Reformed writers made a host of biblical arguments to explain why resisting tyrants is permissible, but I'll mention only one here. Romans 13: 3–4 observes:

> For rulers are not a terror to good works, but to the evil. Wilt thou then not be afraid of the power? do that which is good, and thou shalt have praise of the same. For he is the minister of God to thee for good. But if thou do that which is evil, be afraid; for he beareth not the sword in vain: for he is the minister of God, a revenger to execute wrath upon him that doeth evil.

When a governing authority becomes tyrannical—for instance, by routinely rewarding evil and punishing good—it ceases to be the sort of government described by Romans 13. As such, Christians are under no biblical obligation to obey it, and actively resisting tyranny is best characterized as self-defense, not rebellion.

Active Resistance, Passive Resistance, and Rebellion

The thinkers discussed in this section distinguished between "passive resistance"—i.e., the refusal to obey an ungodly command, and "active resistance"—morally permissible resistance to tyranny, including the use of armed force. They often condemned "rebellion" as being the morally or biblically impermissible resistance to lawful authority. By the American founding, many authors used "active resistance" and "rebellion" or "revolution" interchangeably. A few religious leaders in the American founding held to the pre-Reformation idea that "active resistance" was never biblically justified, but they were a distinct minority.[112]

Some early Reformers sanctioned active resistance only by inferior magistrates (as opposed to "private" men and women—i.e., individuals who did not hold political office). Most famously, John Calvin's *Institutes of the Christian Religion* (first edition, 1536; last revised in 1559), taught that private individuals are not to offer active resistance to tyrants, but he went on to write that

> if there are now any magistrates of the
> people, appointed to restrain the will-
> fulness of kings...I am so far from forbid-
> ding them to withstand, in accordance

> with their duty, the fierce licentious-
> ness of kings, that, if they wink at kings
> who violently fall upon and assault
> the lowly common folk, I declare that
> their dissimulation involves nefarious
> perfidy, because they dishonestly betray
> the freedom of the people, of which they
> know that they have been appointed
> protectors by God's ordinance.[113]

This passage has been understood by most commen-
tators as encouraging lesser magistrates to offer active
resistance—including armed resistance—against a
monarch who becomes a tyrant.[114]

After the last edition of the *Institutes* was published,
Calvin suggested in several places that private citizens
may actively resist tyrants. I think there are very good
reasons to believe he arrived at this position,[115] but even
if he did not, it should be beyond dispute that he did not
embrace the doctrine of "passive obedience and uncondi-
tional submission" to civic authorities, as some scholars
have claimed.[116] At a minimum, Calvin sanctioned and
encouraged active resistance by lesser magistrates. But
the Reformed tradition does not begin and end with
John Calvin; other thinkers, confronted with tyranny as
a political reality and not merely a theoretical problem,
developed their own views on the subject.

By the mid-sixteenth century, most Reformed
thinkers in England and Scotland agreed that the people
themselves have a right, and even a duty, to actively resist
tyrants. For instance, John Ponet (1516–1556), in his *Short
Treatise on Political Power* (1556), contended that private
men should generally not kill tyrants, except

where execution of just punishment
upon tyrants, idolaters, and treacherous
governors is either by the whole state
utterly neglected, or the prince with
the nobility and council conspire the
subversion or alteration of their country
and people.[117]

John Knox (1514–1572) encouraged Scottish nobles to
resist the tyrant Queen Mary, and works like his *Letter
to His Beloved Brethren the Commonality of Scotland* can
be reasonably interpreted as urging private citizens to
actively resist the tyrants if their superiors "be negligent
or yet pretend to maintain tyrants in their tyranny."[118]
Likewise, his friend Christopher Goodman preferred
that active resistance be led by magistrates, but if they
refuse to act, he taught that the people have a duty to
resist tyrants. In his words, if the lesser

Magistrates would wholly despise and
betray the justice and laws of God, you
which are subjects with them shall be
condemned except you maintain and
defend the same laws against them, and
all others to the utmost of your powers,
that is, with all strength, with all your
heart, and with all your soul.[119]

More radically still, George Buchanan (1506–1582)
argued in *The Right of the Kingdom of Scotland* (1579)
that tyrants may be removed by "the whole body of the
people" *and* "every individual citizen."[120]

These arguments helped lay the intellectual foundation for the English Civil War (1642–1651), which joined members of Parliament with those who wanted a more thoroughly reformed Church of England against the Royalists who, it was feared, wanted to return England to the Catholic faith. Early in the conflict, Scotland's Samuel Rutherford (1600–1661) published his important *Lex, Rex*, wherein he argued, "We teach that any private man may kill a tyrant, void of all title.... And if he have not the consent of the people, he is an usurper, for we know no external lawful calling that kings have now, or their family, to the crown, but only the call of the people."[121]

Long before the War for Independence, Reformed Americans had experience resisting tyranny. New England Puritans supported Parliament during the English Civil War, and John Cotton even preached a sermon defending the execution of Charles I.[122] After the Restoration, England attempted to "improve" the governance of the colonies by combining New Jersey, New York, Connecticut, Rhode Island, Massachusetts, and Plymouth into a single administrative unit known as the Dominion of New England (1686–89). The second governor of the new entity, Sir Edmund Andros, immediately made himself unpopular by demanding that a Congregational meeting house in Boston be made available for Anglican services and by restricting town meetings. On April 18, 1689, shortly after news of the Glorious Revolution reached Boston, Puritan civic leaders arrested Andros and returned him to England for trial. The new monarchs and Lords of Trade wisely abandoned the Dominion.

Scholars and activists often assert that the Bible teaches that active resistance to tyranny is unbiblical, but that this was not a problem for America's founders because they relied upon John Locke's *Second Treatise* (1689) rather than the Bible.[123] However, note that *every* work I have discussed up to this point was published before the *Second Treatise*. Every major Reformed thinker prior to Locke agreed that inferior magistrates could justly resist rulers who became tyrants. By the English Civil War, most Calvinists had come to embrace the idea that if inferior magistrates did not resist tyranny, it was permissible for private individuals to do so.

I've emphasized the development of Reformed resistance theory because this theological tradition was so influential in late eighteenth-century America. In his magisterial history of religion in America, Sydney Ahlstrom observed that the Reformed tradition was "the religious heritage of three-fourths of the American people in 1776."[124] Similarly, Yale historian Harry Stout states that prior to the War for Independence "the vast majority of colonists were Reformed or Calvinist."[125] When Parliament and the Crown began acting as tyrants (at least from the patriot perspective), Americans had at their disposal a robust tradition of Biblical and theological arguments justifying active resistance to tyranny from which they could draw.

The connection between Reformed resistance theory and the patriots' cause is not an invention of contemporary scholars. Key participants in the conflict drew direct lines between the tradition and the rebellion. For instance, in 1787 John Adams wrote that John Ponet's *Short Treatise on Political Power* (1556) contains "all the essential principles of liberty, which were afterwards dilated on by Sidney and Locke." He also noted the significance of Stephanus Junius Brutus' *Vindiciae Contra Tyrannos*.[126] Later in life, Adams wrote, "I love and revere the memories of Huss, Wickliff, Luther, Calvin,

Zwingli, Melancton, and all the other Reformers, how muchsoever I may differ from them all in many theological metaphysical & philosophical points. As you justly observe, without their great exertions & severe sufferings, the USA had never existed."[127]

The patriots received almost universal support from Reformed ministers.[128] This support was noted by the other side, as suggested by the loyalist Peter Oliver who railed against the "black Regiment, *the dissenting Clergy*, who took so active a part in the Rebellion."[129] King George himself reportedly referred to the War for Independence as "a Presbyterian Rebellion."[130] From the English perspective, British Major Harry Rooke was correct when he confiscated a presumably Calvinist book from an American prisoner and remarked that "[i]t is your G-d Damned Religion of this Country that ruins the Country; Damn your religion."[131]

Some Christians continue to believe that the Bible prohibits active resistance even to the most tyrannical governments. However, even these believers should concede that America's founders were drawing from a long tradition of biblical and theological arguments that viewed such resistance to be permissible. Even so, we must still consider whether resistance in *this* case was justified. The Christian just war tradition helps us to answer this question.[132]

The Just War Tradition

Just war thinkers maintain that the tradition of which we are a part does not consist of a checklist, but for reasons of space I must present it as such. As the tradition has developed, a war is considered to be justly entered (*jus ad bellum*) if:

1. There is a just cause;
2. It is declared by the proper authority;
3. Those going to war have the right intent;
4. There is a reasonable chance of success;
5. The end is proportionate to the means;
6. It is the last resort.

Just war thinkers are also interested in how wars are fought, *jus in bello*, and how they are ended, *jus post bellum*. I consider only the question of whether the patriots were justified in actively resisting Great Britain. Those few scholars who have addressed questions of *jus in bello* in this conflict have concluded, in John Roche's words, that "the Continental Army conducted itself in an exemplary fashion, not only strictly adhering to *jus in bello* criteria, but frequently exceeding the eighteenth-century 'custom and usages of war.'"[133] Roche addresses *jus post bellum* considerations as well, although briefly, as "it is a recent invention that had no contemporary parallel in 1783" (the year the War for Independence officially ended).[134]

American patriots gave a host of reasons explaining why they were justified in resisting Great Britain. Chief among their concerns were Parliament's attempt to tax the colonists to raise revenue. This complaint is often misunderstood, so I'll discuss it at some length. I then turn to the neglected concern that Parliament was about to restrict the civil and religious liberty of non-Anglicans. Finally, I'll mention briefly other issues and explore the Declaration of Independence, before addressing to the questions of whether the war was declared by the proper authority and was the last resort.

Just Cause:
No Taxation without Representation

Those who deny or question the justice of the patriots' decision to go to war often assert that their cause was unjust. Patriot complaints about the Sugar Act, the Stamp Act, and the Townshend Duties are unpersuasive (the argument goes) because these taxes were—in Gregg Frazer's words—"miniscule," "minimal," and "slight."[135] Indeed, American colonists were asked to pay far less in taxes than were English citizens.[136] These facts are all true, but they miss the point. The patriots' complaint was not that they were too heavily taxed—it was that Parliament had *no* authority to tax them.[137]

American patriots firmly believed the British constitutional maxim that there can be no taxation without representation—a principle that can be traced back to the Magna Charta (1215): "No scutage [tax] or aid shall be imposed on our kingdom, unless by common counsel of our kingdom...."[138] American colonists were not represented in Parliament; therefore, Parliament could not tax Americans. In the words of one of the most prominent students of the War for American Independence, Parliament's attempt to raise revenue from the colonists were "surprising, considering that the Americans were unrepresented in Parliament, an agency which took its beginnings from the right of the people to be taxed only by their own representatives."[139]

In 1763, most colonists in British North America were proud to be part of the British Empire. They were represented in their local legislatures, which in turn taxed them to provide for the general welfare. The English Parliament had the right to tax people in England, but not citizens elsewhere in the empire. Most Americans conceded that Parliament could pass *external* taxes, e.g., duties on imported goods to pay the expenses of customs officials and the like, but Parliament had no right to tax the colonists *internally*, or to pass external taxes merely to raise revenue.

In 1764—to help repay the debt incurred in the French and Indian War—Parliament enacted the Sugar Act, which attempted, for the first time, to raise tax revenue from American colonists. A number of individuals and colonial bodies immediately objected that the act was unconstitutional. The following year, Parliament passed the Stamp Act, which again attempted to raise revenue from the American colonists—but this time by an *internal* tax. Again, many Americans objected strongly to these measures on constitutional grounds, perhaps none so eloquently as James Otis in his pamphlet "The Rights of the British Colonies Asserted and Proved" (1765).

In 1765, nine colonies sent delegates to the Stamp Act Congress in New York City. These leaders adopted the "Declaration of Rights and Grievances," petitioned both Parliament and the King, and agreed to boycott British goods.[140] Economic pressure led Parliament to repeal the Stamp Act in March 1766, but it immediately passed the Declaratory Act, which asserted that Parliament has "full power and authority...to bind the colonies and the people of America...in all cases whatsoever," a claim Americans found to be both remarkable and dangerous.[141] Many patriots understood Parliament to be claiming that there were no constitutional or other limitations on its power, which in their minds was a recipe for tyranny.

Before progressing, it is worth noting that some important English political leaders supported the colonists' constitutional arguments. For instance, in a 1766 speech in Parliament, former (and future) Prime Minister William Pitt commended the colonies for their resistance to unconstitutional taxes and argued that "the Stamp Act should be repealed absolutely, totally, and immediately; that the reason for the repeal should be assigned, because it was founded on [the] erroneous principle...[that Parliament can] take money out of their [American colonists'] pockets without their consent."[142] Pitt also opposed including the phrase "in all cases whatsoever" in the Declaratory Act.[143] A decade after Pitt made these comments, the Aldermen of London petitioned the King on behalf of their American cousins, observing that "no people can be bound to surrender their rights and liberties as a return for protection."[144] Finally, in 1791, the great conservative thinker Edmund Burke, referring to himself in the third person, observed that

> he always firmly believed that they [American colonists] were purely on the defensive in that rebellion. He considered the Americans as standing at that time, and in that controversy, in the same relation to England, as England did to king James the Second, in 1688. He believed, that they had taken up arms from one motive only; that is our attempting to tax them without their consent; to tax them

for the purposes of maintaining civil and military establishments. If this attempt of ours could have been practically established, he thought with them, that their assemblies would become totally useless; that under the system of policy which was then pursued, the Americans could have no sort of security for their laws or liberties, or for any part of them; and, that the very circumstance of *our* freedom would have augmented the weight of *their* slavery (emphasis original).[145]

In 1767, Parliament, relying on the distinction between internal and external taxes, passed a series of duties known as the Townshend Acts. American patriots opposed them because they were aimed at raising revenue but also because leading attorneys—including James Wilson, John Adams, and Thomas Jefferson—had concluded that Parliament had no authority to pass either internal *or external* taxes on American colonists.[146] Another wave of boycotts led Parliament to repeal most of the Townshend duties in 1770, except for the duty on tea. Parliament kept this tax to prove that it had the authority to tax the colonists, but this tactic resulted in the Boston Tea Party. Parliament responded to the Tea Party by passing the Coercive Acts, a series of punishing acts that included closing Boston harbor.[147]

Patriots from north to south were alarmed by Parliament's increasingly aggressive behavior, and every colony but one sent delegates to the First Continental Congress in 1774. This intercontinental political body rapidly passed a host of petitions and addresses to, among others, the people of Great Britain, other British colonies, and the King. These documents reiterate the constitutional arguments discussed above, as well as documenting the violation of other rights, some of which will be discussed below.

Matters escalated when the British General Gage sent troops to Lexington and Concord to seize military supplies in 1775. American patriots defended themselves, and the War for American Independence began. Regardless of who fired the first shot, American patriots were convinced that they could justly resist an armed force whose mission was to disarm citizens.[148] Edmund Burke agreed that England was the aggressor in this conflict, and that the patriots were fighting a defensive war.[149]

Before continuing, let me concede that the constitutional debates discussed in this section are complicated, and it is certainly the case that good, well-meaning people can disagree on these matters. My contention is not that the patriots were indisputably correct—just that their arguments were more than plausible. Indeed, as we have seen, both William Pitt and Edmund Burke agreed that their constitutional claims were valid at the time, and Queen Elizabeth II seemed to agree in a 1976 speech (discussed below). Legal historians differ on this question, but prominent scholars, including Charles McIlwain, Barbara Black, and John Phillip Reid, make a persuasive case that the patriots were correct.[150]

Even so, one might object, the taxes were so light that they did not justify armed resistance. To understand why a constitutional point like this matters, consider for a moment how Americans should react if the United Nations required every American citizen to pay a tax of one dollar a year. This is a trifling sum, yet I hope no one would pay it because the U.N. has no authority to levy taxes on the American people. As James Madison wrote in his Memorial and Remonstrance:

> it is proper to take alarm at the first experiment on our liberties. We hold this prudent jealousy to be the first duty of citizens, and one of the noblest characteristics of the late Revolution. The free men of America did not wait till usurped power had strengthened itself by exercise, and entangled the question in precedents. They saw all the consequences in the principle, and they avoided the consequences by denying the principle.... [T]he same authority which can force a citizen to contribute three pence only of his property for the support of any one establishment, may force him to confirm to any other establishment in all cases whatsoever.[151]

A government that can pass a small tax can pass larger ones and also infringe upon other liberties. A small, unconstitutional tax of this nature can and should be resisted.

In this hypothetical scenario, Americans would not be justified in launching a military assault on the United

Nations the moment it passed the tax. America's ambassador to the U.N. should argue against the measure, and America's civic leaders, especially elected national officials, should protest as well. If the U.N. persisted in its action, America might escalate its response: for example, refusing to pay its dues and perhaps boycotting the body. But, if the United Nations eventually sent troops in blue helmets to seize America's military bases and impose its will on the nation, there is little doubt that the nation would be justified in defending itself. That the initial tax was "miniscule," "minimal," and "slight" would be completely irrelevant.[152]

Just Cause: Religious Liberty

Among the most overlooked causes of the War for Independence were the threats to religious liberty perceived by many colonists. To grasp their concerns, we must remember that 84 percent of America's colonists were considered by the Crown to be religious dissenters. King George III was the head of the Church of England. This denomination was the established church in four New York counties and in Maryland, Virginia, Georgia, and the Carolinas. However, even in these colonies, a majority of citizens were not members of the Church of England (also referred to as Anglicans). Indeed, only 16 percent of all Americans identified with this denomination.[153] The Congregational church was established in Massachusetts, Connecticut, and New Hampshire, while Delaware, New Jersey, Pennsylvania, and Rhode Island had no official church.

Many of America's religious dissenters, or their ancestors, came to America so that they could worship God according to the dictates of conscience. They feared that Parliament and the Crown might one day decide to insist that all British colonists should be taxed to support the Church of England and that dissenters would be discriminated against, as they were in England (Quakers, for instance, could not serve in Parliament until 1832).[154] Some Anglicans argued that an Anglican bishop should be sent to North America and that ecclesiastical courts should be created. The possibility that a bishop might be sent to America had been debated throughout the eighteenth century, most recently sparking a pamphlet war in 1763. The Stamp Act, passed two years later, had contained an obscure reference to courts "exercising ecclesiastical jurisdiction within the said colonies."[155] This was taken by partisans on both sides to imply that a bishop would be sent shortly and that for the first-time, ecclesiastical courts would operate in the American colonies.

Reformed Americans, especially, had vivid memories of persecution their English Puritan ancestors had suffered under Anglican leaders such as Archbishop William Laud (1573–1645). Connecticut's Roger Sherman, for instance, recalled in a 1768 letter that "many of the first inhabitants of these colonies were obliged to seek an asylum among savages in this wilderness in order to escape the tyranny of Archbishop Laud and others of his stamp.... We dread the consequences as oft we think of this danger [ecclesiastical tyranny]."[156] However, it was not just New England Calvinists who objected to the possibility of a bishop. As Thomas Kidd, one of the best students of religion in the founding, has put it, "fear of British power and the tradition of local control of churches ultimately made southerners just a resistant as northerners to increased Anglican power."[157] Long after the war, John Adams observed that "the apprehension of Episcopacy contributed...as much as any other cause, to arouse the attention not only of the inquiring mind, but of the common people, and urge them to close thinking on the constitutional authority of parliament over the colonies."[158]

These fears may seem excessive today, but to an eighteenth-century dissenter, they made perfect sense. Dissenters had often struggled against unfriendly governments, and New England Puritans had come to America precisely because they were unable to reform the Church of England. Throughout the eighteenth century, some American Anglicans continued to argue that most dissenting churches were not "true" churches because their ministers had not been ordained by bishops. The extent to which Anglican leaders in England supported the plan to send a bishop has been extensively debated by scholars, but there is little reason to doubt that dissenters genuinely feared an Anglican episcopate. Ill-conceived actions by the Church of England, such as founding a "mission" in Cambridge, Massachusetts, in 1759, did little to calm their fears.[159]

If the Anglican church was viewed with suspicion by dissenters, the Roman Catholic church was viewed as Satan's handmaiden by the vast majority of American Protestants in the era. As such, many Americans were stunned when Parliament passed the Quebec Act of 1774. From England's perspective, this innocuous piece of legislation simply provided for the efficient governing of territory won from France after the Seven Years' War. However, the act extended the colony of Quebec into what is now the American Midwest, permitted the use

"An Attempt to Land a Bishop in America." *Political Register*, September 1768. This 1768 political cartoon published in an American newspaper represents an Anglican bishop who is not allowed to disembark in America because of a rioting mob. Most notably, he is about to be hit in the head by a copy of *Calvin's Works*, which presumably had been thrown by a protestor.

of French civil law, and allowed Catholics to freely practice their faith and take oaths without reference to Protestantism. To many Protestants, these steps constituted a significant retreat for the kingdom of God in North

America and profound victories for "Papists" and arbitrary government. Connecticut minister Samuel Sherwood reflected the views of many Calvinists when he interpreted the Quebec Act as attempting "the establishment of popery" and as part of a pattern of "violent and cruel attempts of a tyrannical and persecuting power," the main goal of which was the destruction of Protestant Christianity.[160]

In 1774, Congress approved a bill of rights and list of grievances, which among many other complaints, included Parliament's

> establishing the Roman catholic religion in the province of Quebec, abolishing the equitable system of English laws, and erecting a tyranny there, to the great danger, from so total a dissimilarity of religion, law, and government of the neighboring British colonies, by the assistance of those whose blood and treasure the said country was conquered from France.[161]

Similarly, when Congress appealed directly to the people of Great Britain, it contended that Parliament was

> not authorized by the constitution to establish a religion, fraught with sanguinary and impious tenets, or, to erect an arbitrary form of government, in any quarter of the globe. These rights, we, as well as you, deem sacred. And yet sacred

as they are, they have, with many others
been repeatedly and flagrantly violated.[162]

These quotations, and many more could be given,
highlight issues that are only vaguely represented in
the Declaration of Independence. Many delegates to the
first Continental Congress were profoundly concerned
about the establishment of the Catholic faith in Quebec,
and they often spoke specifically as "Protestants."[163] By
contrast, the Declaration of Independence mentions
only "abolishing the free System of English Laws in a
neighboring Province." This is because a critical audience for the Declaration was Roman Catholic France.
The eventual intervention of France on the patriots' side
did much to diminish the vehement anti-Catholicism of
many Americans in this era, but waves of "Papist" immigrants in the nineteenth century spurred a resurgence of
anti-Catholicism.

Some patriot leaders were more concerned about
these perceived threats to religious liberty than others.
It is fair to say that Southern Anglican gentlemen, such
as Washington, Jefferson, and Madison, lost little sleep
over the possibility that a bishop might be sent to North
America. There is also little doubt that the fears of non-Anglicans, especially Calvinists, were exaggerated. By themselves, these threats to the sacred right of conscience
would not justify active resistance to Great Britain.
But when combined with other assaults on the colonists' civil and religious liberty, they reinforced the fear
that Parliament and the Crown had become tyrannical.

Just Cause: Other Violations and the (In)action of King George III

American patriots did not deny that they had any allegiance to Great Britain. They acknowledged that they should obey the Crown but contended that this was a reciprocal obligation. The colonists had a duty to subject themselves to the King because he protected them. Among their responses to Parliament's abuses were several appeals to the Crown for protection. When King George III refused to receive their petitions and, in fact, declared the colonists to be excluded from his protection, in their minds, their obligation to the Crown was dissolved.[164] In the words of the Reverend Moses Mather, "[t]he king by withdrawing his protection and levying war upon us has discharged us of our allegiance, and of all obligations to obedience. For protection and subjection are mutual, and cannot subsist apart."[165]

When Americans read the Declaration of Independence, we are naturally drawn to the beautiful and important words in the first two paragraphs, especially the observation that

> We hold these truths to be self-evident:
> that all men are created equal; that
> they are endowed by their Creator with
> certain unalienable rights; that among
> these are life, liberty and the pursuit of
> happiness. That, to secure these rights,
> governments are instituted among men,
> deriving their just powers from the
> consent of the governed.[166]

Abraham Lincoln, along with many others, argued that America was founded upon these majestic principles.[167] Note that the rights referred to here are natural rights—that is, rights possessed by all people at all times and in all places. Natural rights arguments play an important role in many of the colonists' arguments, but for reasons of space, here I focus primarily on the constitutional arguments.

The bulk of the Declaration of Independence is a legal argument showing that "the history of the present King of Great Britain is a history of repeated injuries and usurpations, all having in direct object the establishment of an absolute tyranny."[168] Parliament is not mentioned, as the patriots had thoroughly convinced themselves that they had no obligation whatsoever to this body. In their minds, the only connection they had to the British Empire was to the King, and he had forfeited his right to be obeyed by repeatedly violating the colonies' constitutional rights. Indeed, the Declaration lists at least twenty-seven specific violations, including, in addition to those already mentioned:

—obstructing the administration of justice
—making judges dependent on his will alone
—quartering large bodies of armed troops among us
—depriving citizens of the benefits of trial by jury
—transporting large armies of foreign mercenaries to complete the works of death, desolation and tyranny

Some of these offenses are more serious than others, but collectively, they constituted—at least in the patriots' minds—that "a long train of abuses and usurpation, pursing invariably the same object, evinces a design to reduce them under absolute despotism." As such, they felt justified in exercising their "right" and "duty" to throw off such government, and provide new guards for their future security."[169]

In hindsight, some scholars have made a reasonable case that some patriot fears were overblown. For instance, there appears to have been little support for sending a bishop to America, and—if one had been sent—it seems unlikely that he would have attempted to curtail the ability of religious dissenters to worship God as they saw fit. But the patriots did not have the benefit of hindsight. Statesmen must act on the information they have at a particular point in time, and, all things considered, it is more than reasonable to conclude that America's civic leaders had just cause to resist what they perceived to be England's unconstitutional and unjust acts.

Proper Authority, Last Resort, and Reasonable Chance of Success

Three other arguments must be briefly addressed. First, some have contended that the war for American Independence was not declared by the proper authority. Such authorities, they contend, must be clearly and constitutionally empowered to resist a tyrant.[170] For instance, in our current constitutional order, Congress has the power to impeach and convict a president who commits high crimes. Neither the colonial governments nor the national bodies created by them (e.g., the Stamp Act Congress or the Continental Congress) clearly had such authority. If the premise of this argument is correct, then critics would have a point. However, a good case can be made that colo-

nial legislatures and colony-wide congresses were inferior magistrates of the sort required by Calvin and other
Reformers. Even if they were not, by the late eighteenth
century, virtually all Protestants had come to agree that,
if inferior magistrates did not actively resist a tyrant, the
people could do so on their own authority.[171] This conviction was only reinforced by John Locke's *Second Treatise*,
a work that helped spread Reformed resistance theory to
non-Calvinists.

Was war the last resort for the patriots? Answering
this sort of prudential question is always complicated.
For more than a decade, from the Stamp Act Congress
(1765) to the Declaration of Independence (1776), colonial
leaders met and attempted to redress their grievances in
a peaceful manner. They petitioned Parliament and the
Crown and pled their case with the British people. They
engaged in non-violent resistance and made every effort
to resolve their differences with Great Britain. In 1763,
most Americans were proud British subjects. It was only
after a "long train of abuses," which included being fired
upon by British soldiers, that they resorted to armed
resistance. It was reasonable for patriots to conclude that
nonviolent remedies had been exhausted and that they
were justified in actively resisting British tyranny.[172]

Some have suggested that the American colonies
could have negotiated independence, just as other British
colonies did later. However, this possibility assumes that
Great Britain learned nothing from its disputes with the
American colonies. Queen Elizabeth II disagreed. In
1976, she remarked:

> We lost the American colonies because
> we lacked the statesmanship to know

the time and the manner of yielding what is impossible to keep. But the lesson was learned. In the next century and a half, we kept more closely to the principles of Magna Carta, which has been the common heritage of both our countries. We learned to respect the right of others to govern themselves in their own way. This was the outcome of experience learned the hard way in 1776. Without that great act in the cause of liberty performed in Independence Hall two hundred years ago, we could never have transformed our Empire into a Commonwealth.[173]

If the American colonies had not stood up for their rights, perhaps Parliament and the Crown would have become more tyrannical. Queen Elizabeth acknowledged that America's active resistance paved the way for other colonies to achieve independence through peaceful means. Also note that she implicitly acknowledges that Parliament violated "the principles of the Magna Carta" and the "right of others to govern themselves." If the Queen of England can admit these mistakes, one would think American college professors could as well.

War should be entered into only if there is a reasonable chance of success. Again, this is a prudential question that is very difficult to answer before a conflict begins. However, we know that the War for American Independence ends with a victory by the American colonies, so it seems more than reasonable that they had a reasonable chance of success. Not to be deterred by such inconvenient facts, John Keown suggests that "it remains doubtful whether the rebels had a reasonable prospect of success when hostilities broke out."[174] Yet General Washington and other patriot leaders understood that it was not necessary to win the war, but simply not to lose it. They recognized that Great Britain would eventually grow weary of the conflict, and that there was every reason to be believe that France could be enticed to enter the war on the patriot side. History proved them to be correct.

Conclusion

Reasonable Christians can disagree about whether active resistance to tyrannical authority is ever justified and, if it is, who should lead it. Morally serious citizens can, and do, differ as to whether entering into a particular conflict is justified or not. I hope this chapter has made it clear that America's founders made reasonable biblical and moral arguments that tyrannical authority may be actively resisted. This chapter has shown that they had legitimate concerns that Parliament and the King were acting in a tyrannical fashion. After more than a decade of resisting these actions through petitions, boycotts, and other non-violent means, they concluded that active resistance, and eventually separation from Great Britain, was justified.

The War for American Independence was fought to guarantee the freedom and equality of American citizens. Patriots believed that actively resisting tyrannical authority was biblically permissible—perhaps even a biblical requirement—and they were confident that their resistance was just. The conflict produced the Declaration of Independence, which includes one of the greatest expressions of the fundamental principles upon which America was founded:

> We hold these truths to be self-evident: that all men are created equal; that they are endowed by their Creator with certain unalienable rights; that among these are life, liberty and the pursuit of happiness. That, to secure these rights, governments are instituted among men, deriving their just powers from the consent of the governed.[175]

To be sure, not everyone in what became the United States of America was free and equal. All men and women are created equal and have a right to be free, but far too many Americans were denied these basic rights—especially African Americans. It is to the grave injustice of American slavery that we must now turn.

CHAPTER THREE

America's Founders and Slavery

The *New York Times*'s *1619 Project* is a series of articles published in 2019 to mark the four hundredth anniversary of the first enslaved Africans to arrive in America. Jake Silverstein's introduction to the series claims that slavery

> is sometimes referred to as the country's original sin, but it is more than that: It is the country's very origin. Out of slavery — and the anti-black racism it required — grew nearly everything that has truly made America exceptional: its economic might, its industrial power, its electoral system, its diet and popular music, the inequities of its public health and education, its astonishing penchant for violence, its income inequality, the example it sets for the world as a land of freedom and equality, its slang, its legal system and the endemic racial fears and hatreds that continue to plague it to this day. The seeds of all that were

planted long before our official birth date, in 1776, when the men known as our founders formally declared independence from Britain.[176]

These are powerful claims. Is it really the case that slavery explains "nearly everything that has truly made America exceptional"?

In a similar vein, Mark Galli, then-editor of the influential magazine *Christianity Today*, asked: "Can we in any way, shape, or form say that America was founded on Christian principles when its very existence and prosperity were set on a foundation of unimaginable cruelty to millions of other human beings?" He answered this question with a resounding "No!"[177] The foundation of which he speaks is the oppression of Native Americans and African Americans. I address only the issue of slavery in this chapter.

America's founders are regularly criticized for being racist slave owners. This criticism is not unwarranted, but it is overly simplistic.[178] Some of America's founders participated in the evils of slavery, but most did not. Furthermore, many of them were motivated by their Christian convictions to take concrete steps to put this vile institution on the road to extinction.

American Slavery in Context

Slavery dates back to the dawn of human history. It has been practiced in every region, and although it is currently illegal in almost every country, scholars and activists estimate that there are as many as 46 million enslaved people today.[179]

Slavery existed in America well before 1619 because Native Americans enslaved other Native Americans.[180] The first enslaved Africans were brought to North America in 1619, but there were already enslaved Africans elsewhere in the New World.[181] Indeed, even the *1619 Project* recognizes that of the 12.5 million Africans kidnapped from their homes and brought to North and South America, only 400,000 of them—about 3.2 percent—came to what we now call the United States.[182] Most were taken to the Caribbean or Brazil. 400,000 stolen humans are 400,000 too many; my point is simply that American colonists were not uniquely evil—they were participating in a practice that was widespread around the globe.[183]

Great Britain's North American colonies were not unusual in permitting slavery. What *was* unique is that when the Massachusetts captain James Smith kidnapped two West Africans and brought them to Boston in 1645, the General Court considered charging him with "man-stealing" (Exodus 21:16). The Court decided not to try Captain Smith because his offense took place outside of the court's jurisdiction, but it ordered the two men to be freed and returned them to Africa at the colony's expense.[184]

The Puritans prohibited slavery except in the case of "lawful captives taken in just wars, and such strangers as willingly sell themselves, or are sold to us."[185] They eventually followed Jamestown in permitting enslaved Africans in New England, but slavery was never widespread in the region. In 1700, enslaved Africans accounted for 1.7 percent of New England's population.[186] Even so, in that same year, the Puritan minister Samuel Sewall published the first antislavery tract in North America: *The Selling of Joseph: A Memorial.*

What Does the Bible Say About Slavery?

Any discussion of Christianity and slavery must acknowledge that the Bible seems to permit the institution. In the Old Testament, slavery is treated as an acceptable practice (e.g., Exodus 20:10; 21:1-32), although distinct limits are placed upon how Jewish slaves were to be treated, redeemed, and eventually freed (Leviticus 25). Although Israelites were permitted to purchase foreigners as slaves (Leviticus 25: 44–46), Deuteronomy 23: 15–16 prohibits God's people from returning slaves who escape from their foreign masters.

The New Testament seems to allow for slavery as well. For instance, in Ephesians 6:5 the Apostle Paul wrote, "slaves, be obedient to those who are your masters according to the flesh, with fear and trembling, in the sincerity of your heart, as to Christ" (NASB). The Greek word δοῦλοι is sometimes translated as "servants" or "bondservants," but it is clearly referring to slaves. The Apostle Peter offered a similar admonition in I Peter 2: 18–19, and, in the book of Philemon, Paul sends Onesimus, an escaped slave who converted to Christianity, back to his master Philemon (albeit with a strong suggestion that Onesimus be freed).

Although some biblical passages seem to permit slavery, abolitionists contended that it does not support the race-based chattel slavery that was practiced in America. Instead, they argued that the Old Testament allows a form of slavery that closely resembles voluntary servitude or temporary servitude to pay a debt. As well, they often insisted that verses requiring slaves to obey their masters were binding only in specific contexts. They should be classified with a passage such as I Corinthians 11:5, which seems to require that women cover their heads while praying. Some Christians continue to believe that this verse is normative today, but most do not. In the same way, someone might reasonably conclude that at one time the Bible required slaves to obey their masters, but no longer.

Abolitionists also pointed to biblical passages that seem to condemn slavery. As noted, some Puritans argued that the African slave trade violated the biblical prohibition against "man-stealing" (Exodus 21:16). At a more foundational level, Genesis 1:27 states that all humans are created in the image of God. Christian leaders have long taught that this means, among other things, that all humans must be treated with dignity and respect. Although it might be possible for a slave owner to treat an enslaved person in this manner, in practice, slavery seldom leads to such results. Accordingly, it follows that this institution should be abolished.

In the late eighteenth and early nineteenth centuries, some "scientific" racists taught that blacks and whites were separate races. Orthodox Christians had very little patience with these arguments, as they believed that all humans descended from one couple: Adam and Eve. In addition to Genesis, opponents of the multiple origins theory often cited Acts 17:26: "And [God] hath made of one blood all nations of men for to dwell on all the face of the earth, and hath determined the times before appointed, and the bounds of their habitation."[187] Popular as well was Galatians 3:28: "There is neither Jew nor Greek, there is neither bond nor free, there is neither male nor female: for ye are all one in Christ Jesus."

"The Slave Bible"

Enslaved Africans took comfort in the story of Moses leading the Jewish people out of bondage in Egypt. This account was so powerful that slave owners purchased special Bibles for slaves that conspicuously removed this story. Despite these "Slave Bibles," the Exodus story continued to be told and was featured prominently in African American Spirituals such as "Go Down, Moses," which includes stanzas such as:

I believe without a doubt:
Let my people go!

A Christian has a right to shout,
Let my people go![188]

When the Reverend Dr. Martin Luther King, Jr. was awarded the Nobel Peace Prize in 1964, he observed in his Nobel Lecture:

Oppressed people cannot remain oppressed forever. The yearning for freedom eventually manifests itself. The Bible tells the thrilling story of how Moses stood in Pharaoh's court centuries ago and cried, "Let my people go." This is a kind of opening chapter in a continuing story.[189]

It seems obvious to most twenty-first century Christians that slavery, at least as practiced in America, is unbiblical. I agree. At the same time, historical humility requires us to see that the Bible does not clearly and unequivocally condemn slavery. That some founders did not actively oppose the institution or free their own slaves does not mean that they were not Christians or that they did not accept the Bible's authority.

The Founders and Slavery

Let's turn now to what America's founders said and did about slavery. We should perhaps first note that the vast majority of white Americans never owned a slave.[190] Civic leaders tended to be wealthier than the average American and so were more likely to own slaves. Of the fifty-six men to sign the Declaration, forty-one were slave owners at some point in their lives. At the same time, only twenty-five of the fifty-five delegates to the Constitutional Convention ever owned an enslaved person. Below I discuss the antislavery activity of founders who never owned slaves, but I'll begin with the hard cases: founders who enslaved other human beings.[191]

No founder defended slavery as a positive good, and even many slave owners were coming to oppose the institution. For instance, John Dickinson—"Penman of the Revolution" and framer of the Constitution— was at one time the largest slave owner in Delaware. He conditionally freed his slaves in 1777, and manumitted (freed) them completely in 1786.[192] James Wilson of Pennsylvania, on the other hand, only owned one slave who served as a household servant. He voluntarily freed him in 1794.[193]

John Jay, the nation's first chief justice, owned several slaves but manumitted them all. When serving in New York's constitutional convention of 1777, he attempted but failed to ban slavery in the state. Jay later helped found and served as president of the New York Manumission Society. (Other members of this society included Alexander Hamilton, Noah Webster, Egbert Benson (a member of the first federal Congress), and governors George Clinton and Daniel Tomkins.) In 1799, when serving as governor of New York, Jay signed a law gradually abolishing slavery in the state.[194]

Benjamin Franklin was a member of the five-person committee that drafted the Declaration of Independence. He owned a handful of slaves who worked as household servants between 1735 and 1781. Through the influence of the Quaker Anthony Benezet and other abolitionists, he came to oppose slavery and freed the last of his "servants" in 1781. He joined the Philadelphia-based Society for Promoting the Abolition of Slavery and the Relief of Negroes Unlawfully Held in Bondage in 1785 and became its president in 1787. In 1790, he signed a petition which was sent to Congress requesting that slavery be abolished throughout the United States.[195]

Benjamin Rush, an important but neglected founder, graduated from the College of New Jersey (now Princeton), apprenticed as a doctor, and then went to Scotland to study medicine at the University of Edinburgh. Upon his return to America in 1768, he published an essay against slavery entitled "An Address to the Inhabitants of the British Settlements in America, upon Slave-Keeping." Among other things, he believed slavery to be a national sin:

> Remember that national crimes require national punishments, and without declaring what punishment awaits this evil, you may venture to assure them that it cannot pass with impunity, unless God shall cease to be just or merciful.[196]

Rush went on to serve in the Continental Congress and was a signer of the Declaration of Independence. In 1788, he was a leader in Pennsylvania's ratification convention, where he supported the Constitution. Despite his pamphlet condemning slavery, Rush purchased a slave named William Grubber in 1776. He still owned the slave when he joined the Pennsylvania abolition society in 1784, although he finally freed him in 1794.

To their credit, the slave-owning founders discussed thus far freed their slaves. Some slave-owning founders criticized the institution but did not free their slaves. George Washington, for instance, wrote in a letter to Robert Morris that "there is not a man living who wishes more sincerely than I do, to see a plan adopted for the abolition of it [slavery]."[197] Similarly, James Madison lamented that "[w]e have seen the mere distinction of color made in the most enlightened period of time, a ground for the most oppressive dominion ever exercised by man over man."[198] Another great Virginian, Patrick Henry, wrote to a Quaker who had freed his slaves:

> Is it not amazing that at a time when the rights of humanity are defined and understood with precision, in a country,

> above all others fond of liberty, that in
> such an age and in such a country, we
> find men professing a religion the most
> humane, mild, gentle, and generous,
> adopting a principle [slavery] as repug-
> nant to humanity, as it is inconsis-
> tent with the Bible, and destructive to
> liberty?[199]

Of these three, only Washington freed his slaves, albeit after his death.[200]

If the founders were troubled by slavery, why did many slave-owners not free their slaves? In some cases, state laws made it difficult to do so. In others, slave owners were indebted and so could not free their "property" before satisfying creditors. The likely main reason was that slave owners enjoyed the benefits of slavery so much that they rationalized their participation in it.

Slavery and the Nation's Organic Laws

According to Peter Kolchin, one of the best students of American slavery, "the United States was the first country to take significant (although ultimately limited) action against the peculiar institution [i.e., slavery]."[201] In the late eighteenth century, America's civic leaders passed a series of laws at the national and state levels that they hoped would put slavery on the road to extinction. Let's begin by considering three key documents from this era: the Declaration of Independence (1776), the North-west Ordinance (1787, 1789), and the Constitution of the United States (1788).[202]

Declaration of Independence

The Continental Congress voted for independence on July 2, 1776, and on July 4, 1776, the body approved a declaration of independence. This document was intended to justify America's break from Great Britain to the world. Most relevant for the debate over slavery is the stirring proclamation that

> We hold these truths to be self-evident, that all men are created equal, that they are endowed by their Creator with certain unalienable Rights, that among these are Life, Liberty, and the Pursuit of Happiness.[203]

The Declaration of Independence was a political document with multiple purposes. However, throughout history, Americans have appealed to the principles articulated in it for a variety of purposes, including opposing slavery.

According to the *1619 Project*, "the white men who drafted those words [in the Declaration] did not believe them to be true for the hundreds of thousands of black people in their midst."[204] Similarly, Jemar Tisby asserts that few "political leaders assumed the noble words of the Declaration applied to the enslaved."[205] It is certainly the case that the Declaration did not immediately free any slaves, but many of its authors were troubled by the institution. Four of the members of the committee charged with drafting the Declaration went on to play important roles in opposing slavery. I have already discussed Franklin and will turn shortly to

Roger Sherman and John Adams, but let's begin with its primary drafter: Thomas Jefferson. The Sage of Monticello never freed his slaves, but he did more to oppose slavery than is often realized.[206] Indeed, his draft of the Declaration condemned King George for waging

> cruel war against human nature itself, violating its most sacred rights of life & liberty in the persons of a distant people who never offended him, captivating & carrying them into slavery in another hemisphere, or to incur miserable death in their transportation thither [and] determined to keep open a market where MEN should be bought & sold, he has prostituted his negative for suppressing every legislative attempt to prohibit or to restrain this execrable commerce....[207]

This provision was eventually removed at the insistence of delegates from the deep South, but there is no question that Jefferson was troubled by slavery. The year after he penned the Declaration, he drafted a bill that would have banned the importation of slaves into Virginia.[208] In 1785, he wrote *Notes on the State of Virginia*, a work the historian Kevin Gutzman calls "the most influential antislavery book of his age."[209] In it, he observed with respect to slavery:

> can the liberties of a nation be thought secure when we have removed their only firm basis, a conviction in the minds of the

people that these liberties are of the gift of God? That they are not to be violated but with his wrath? Indeed, I tremble for my country when I reflect that God is just: that his justice cannot sleep for ever: that considering numbers, nature and natural means only, a revolution of the wheel of fortune, an exchange of situation, is among possible events: that it may become probable by supernatural interference! The Almighty has no attribute which can take side with us in such a contest.[210]

Jefferson recognized that slavery was unjust, but in the same work, he contended that emancipation was not a viable solution because of "deep-rooted prejudices entertained by the whites; ten thousand recollections by the blacks of the injuries they have sustained; new provocations; the real distinctions nature has made...."[211] He was convinced that simply manumitting slaves would lead to constant fighting between African Americans and white Americans, if not a race war.[212] Instead, he proposed to free slaves and then ship them "to such place as the circumstances of the time should render most proper." He drafted a bill to achieve this result in Virginia, but it did not become law.[213]

In an 1820 letter, Jefferson reiterated his support for "gradual emancipation and *expatriation*" (emphasis original). The notion that freed slaves should be "colonized" elsewhere was surprisingly popular among Southern leaders, but it was never a realistic possibility. Jefferson likely recognized this fact, which may be why in the same letter he observed that being a slave owner was similar to holding a "wolf by the ears, we can neither hold him, nor safely let him go. Justice is on one scale, and self-preservation on the other."[214] Jefferson understood that slavery was wrong but feared the consequences of emancipating enslaved African Americans. We may rightly criticize his inability to envision ways in which slavery might be ended peacefully, but we should acknowledge the actions he took to oppose the "peculiar institution."

Colonization

The idea of freeing and colonizing former slaves in Africa was supported by numerous Southern leaders. In 1816, James Madison agreed to become the first president of the American Colonization Society. With President James Monroe's support, the Society began transporting freeborn and manumitted African Americans to Liberia in 1822. The capital of this colony, which later became an independent nation, was named Monrovia in honor of President Monroe. Members of the Colonization Society included "future president John Tyler, Henry Clay, John Randolph of Roanoke, John Taylor of Caroline, and various other prominent politicians among its tens of thousands of members."[215] Roughly 12,000 African Americans were transported to West Africa before slavery was finally abolished in the United States. During this time the number of slaves in the South increased from 1,509,904 to 3,950,511, which helps show that colonization was never a feasible plan.[216]

The Declaration of Independence was regularly appealed to by opponents of slavery. Indeed, within a few months of its publication, the African American preacher Lemuel Haynes wrote a pamphlet condemning slavery that begins by quoting the Declaration's powerful claim: "We hold these truths to be self-evident that all men are created equal." Later, relying on the authority of Acts 17:26, he argued that "liberty is equally as precious to a black man, as it is to a white one, and bondage equally as intolerable to the one as it is to the other."[217] Haynes's pamphlet was not published in his lifetime, but many other antislavery tracts were. They regularly appealed to the Declaration.[218]

In his famous 1852 speech "What to the Slave Is the Fourth of July," Frederick Douglass, after describing the evils of slavery, observed that

> notwithstanding the dark picture I have this day presented of the state of the nation, I do not despair of this country. There are forces in operation, which must inevitably work the downfall of slavery. "The arm of the Lord is not shortened," [Isaiah 59:1] and the doom of slavery is certain. I, therefore, leave off where I began, with hope. While drawing encouragement from the Declaration of Independence, the great principles it contains, and the genius of American institutions, my spirit is also cheered by the obvious tendencies of the age.[219]

Sometime after his election in 1860, Abraham Lincoln penned a private set of reflections on the relationship between the Declaration and the Constitution. He observed that the Declaration articulated the principles upon which America was founded and that the Constitution was intended to bring these principles into effect. He concluded his thoughts by using Proverbs 25: 11, "a word fitly spoken is like apples of gold in pictures of silver," to compare the two:

> The assertion of that *principle*, at *that time*, was the word, *"fitly spoken"* which has proved an "apple of gold" to us [the principles of the Declaration]. The *Union*, and the *Constitution*, are the *picture* of *silver*, subsequently framed around it. The picture was made, not to *conceal*, or *destroy* the apple; but to *adorn*, and *preserve* it. The *picture* was made *for* the apple—*not* the apple for the picture (emphasis in original).[220]

Lincoln's Emancipation Proclamation (1863) and his support of the Thirteenth Amendment (1865) did much to help the nation realize the promises of the Declaration. But that is getting ahead of the story.

The Northwest Ordinance

The Confederation Congress is often described as an ineffectual body, but it passed one of the most important laws in American history: the Northwest Ordinance. This statute provided a process for creating states out of the territory historians call the Old Northwest (Ohio, Michigan, Indiana, Illinois, and Wisconsin). It stipulated that new states would enter the union on an equal footing with earlier states, protected religious liberty, and prohibited slavery.

The Northwest Ordinance's antislavery provision was authored by none other than Thomas Jefferson. Jefferson headed the congressional committee that initially considered what would become of the territory. In 1784, it issued a "Report of a Plan of Government for the Western Territory" in Jefferson's handwriting. Among the committee's proposals was that "after the year 1800 of the Christian era, there shall be neither slavery nor involuntary servitude in any of the said states...."[221]

Jefferson's committee report was incorporated into the Land Ordinance of 1785, which was in turn the basis for the Northwest Ordinance (1787). Like the report, the Ordinance stated that there "shall be neither slavery nor involuntary servitude in the said territory."[222] Unlike his report, this provision was effective immediately. As we shall see in the next section, this Ordinance played an important role in convincing antislavery delegates to the Constitutional Convention to support the proposed constitution. In 1789, the first federal Congress reauthorized the Northwest Ordinance.

The United States Constitution

The Constitutional Convention met in Philadelphia during the summer of 1787. Formally convened to amend the Articles of Confederation, the delegates instead drafted and proposed an entirely new constitution. In this section, I consider only the Convention's approach to slavery.

Twenty-five of the fifty-five delegates to the Constitutional Convention owned slaves, but some of these men—including George Mason, Luther Martin, Rufus King, James Madison, Gouverneur Morris, and John Dickinson—criticized the institution during the debates.[223] The Morris family had owned slaves for years, but Gouverneur Morris opposed the practice. As a delegate to New York's constitutional convention of 1777, he moved to abolish slavery because "[t]he rights of human nature and our religion loudly call upon us to dispense the blessings of freedom to all mankind."[224] His motion failed. At the Convention, he declared slavery to be "a nefarious institution...the curse of heaven on the States where it prevailed." [225]

Maryland's Luther Martin, himself a slave owner, proposed allowing Congress to prohibit or tax the importation of slaves because the institution was "inconsistent with the principles of the revolution and dishonorable to the American character."[226] John Rutledge of South Carolina responded to Martin with the remarkable assertion that "religion and humanity had nothing to do with this question—interest alone is the governing principle with nations. The true question at present is whether the Southern states shall or shall not be parties to the Union."[227] Connecticut's Oliver Ellsworth was unwilling to concede Rutledge's relativistic premise, but he was prepared to reject Martin's proposal because the "morality or wisdom of slavery are considerations belonging to the States themselves." Finally, Charles Pinckney concluded this brief exchange by restating Rutledge's point from the perspective of his state: "South Carolina can never receive the plan if it prohibits the slave trade."[228]

Pinckney's comment ended the debate on August 21. The next day, Connecticut's Roger Sherman opened the Convention by suggesting that the delegates leave the clause prohibiting Congress from banning the importation of slaves for twenty years "as it stands":

> He disapproved of the slave trade: yet as the States were now possessed of the right to import slaves, as the public good did not require it to be taken from them, & as it was expedient to have as few objections as possible to the proposed scheme of Government, he thought it best to leave the matter as we find it. He observed that *the abolition of slavery seemed to be going on in the U.S. & that the good sense of the several States would probably by degrees complete it* (emphasis added).[229]

The issue was not resolved that day, but eventually, the delegates agreed to let Congress tax imported slaves up to ten dollars per person and ban the trade as early as 1808.

Many delegates opposed slavery, but they calculated that proposing a constitution that would not be ratified by Southern states would do little to end the institution. One reason they were willing to compromise on the importation of slaves is that only three states—North Carolina, South Carolina, and Georgia—still permitted it; the others prohibited it as a matter of state law. More significantly, many of the delegates were convinced that states would voluntarily abolish slavery. By the summer of 1787, six states had passed gradual manumission acts or ended slavery through judicial decisions.[230]

The hope that slavery was on the road to extinction was stoked when the Confederation Congress enacted the Northwest Ordinance on July 13, 1787. Opponents of slavery were confident that as the nation expanded and new free states were admitted on equal terms with existing states, the power of the few remaining slave states would be diminished. Oliver Ellsworth captured this sentiment well when he observed in the convention that slavery "in time, will not be a speck in our country."[231]

There is no question that the delegates in Philadelphia were aware of the Northwest Ordinance as three of them, William Few, William Pierce, and William Blount, took a break from the Federal Convention to attend the Confederation Congress, which was then meeting in New York City. Their visit provided a quorum that allowed the body to pass the Ordinance. Blount returned to Philadelphia on August 7, and the Ordinance is mentioned twice in Convention documents and debates.[232]

Politics is the art of the possible. Banning slavery was never a realistic option at the time of the Convention, but many delegates desired to at least prohibit the importation of slaves. Yet, South Carolina's Charles Pinckney was undoubtedly correct when he stated that his home state would never ratify a constitution that banned the slave trade or, by extension, slavery.[233] Indeed, a constitution that banned slavery would not have been ratified by any Southern state and thus would not have been ratified. Perhaps the Northern states should have simply gone their own way, leaving the Southern states to form some version of what later became the Confederacy. It is hard to imagine that this alternative would have been better for slaves in the American South.

The men who drafted the Constitution seem to have been ashamed of slavery, as suggested by the absence of that word "slave" and its cognates in the document. Indeed, James Madison "thought it wrong to admit in the Constitution the idea that there could be property in men."[234] It was assumed that the institution would continue, as indicated by the Three-Fifths Compromise (five slaves were counted as three "persons" for the purposes of representation in the House of Representatives) and the Fugitive Slave Clause (which required the return of escaped slaves). More positively, as a result of another compromise the delegates in Philadelphia agreed that Congress could ban the importation of slaves beginning in 1808. At the urging of then-President Jefferson, Congress prohibited the importation of slaves as soon as it was constitutionally possible.[235]

Abolition in the States

Today, when Americans think of laws, we tend to focus on the national government. However, prior to the early twentieth century, a great deal of important legislation continued to be passed by the states. This is particularly true with respect to slavery. Constitutions, statutes, or judicial decisions were made in every state north of Maryland that provided for immediate or gradual emancipation, including: Vermont (1777), Massachusetts (1780), Pennsylvania (1780), New Hampshire (1783), Rhode Island (1784), Connecticut (1784) New York (1799), and New Jersey (1804).[236] The historian Paul J. Polgar observes that between "1790 and 1810, the rate of growth of the free black population in the United States outpaced that of enslaved Americans, making the trend toward black freedom more noteworthy than the spread of chattel bondage."[237] Space constraints prevent me from discussing the manumission efforts in each of these states, but those in three of them are particularly noteworthy.

Pennsylvania

Pennsylvania was founded by the Quaker William Penn in 1681 as a haven for Quakers and other religious dissenters. Penn owned slaves, and the colony permitted slavery, but even while Penn was founding his colony, some Quakers were condemning slavery, and more were doing so by the mid-eighteenth century. Unfortunately for enslaved Africans, the Quakers lost power in the colony during the 1750s. Nevertheless, in 1780 a coalition of Quakers and other Christians were able to pass a gradual manumission act. This act is particularly noteworthy because the legislators explained that when they reflected on God's deliverance from Great Britain:

> we are unavoidably led to a serious and grateful sense of the manifold blessings which we have undeservedly received from the hand of that Being from whom every good and perfect gift cometh [James 1:17]. Impressed with these ideas, we conceive that it is our duty, and we rejoice that it is in our power to extend a portion of that freedom to others, which hath been extended to us; and a release from that state of thralldom to which we ourselves were tyrannically doomed, and from which we have now every prospect of being

delivered. It is not for us to enquire why, in the creation of mankind, the inhabitants of the several parts of the earth were distinguished by a difference in feature or complexion. It is sufficient to know that all are the work of an Almighty Hand....[238]

One does not need to be a Christian to oppose slavery, but in America, virtually all abolitionists were motivated by their Christian convictions.

Connecticut

Roger Sherman was a member of the five-person committee charged with drafting the Declaration of Independence. He also helped draft and/or signed the Declaration and Resolves (1774), the Articles of Association (1774), the Declaration of Independence (1776), the Articles of Confederation (1777, 1778), the Constitution (1787), and the Bill of Rights (1789). According to David Brian Robertson, the "political synergy between Madison and Sherman...[at the Constitutional Convention] may have been necessary for the Constitution's adoption."[239]

After America declared independence, many states revised their laws. Connecticut asked Roger Sherman and Richard Law to do so in 1783. They worked on their project throughout the summer and fall, and the General Assembly reviewed their work, accepted, rejected, and amended their proposals, and approved the new state code in January of 1784.[240] Among their revisions was an act to amend Connecticut's statute on slavery to manumit children born to slaves after March

1, 1784, when they reached the age of twenty-five. In the same year the law was approved, Sherman published an essay defending the rights of Native Americans, where he quoted Acts 17:26: "That God hath made of one blood, all nations of the earth, and hath determined the bounds of their habitation."[241]

Connecticut's gradual emancipation act of 1784 did not immediately free any slaves, yet it sped the decline of slavery in the state. Between 1790 and 1800, the number of slaves dropped from 2,764 to 951. Some slaves may have been shipped out of state; a practice the legislature prohibited in 1788 with respect to children entitled to freedom at age twenty-five, and for all slaves in 1792.

Massachusetts

Like Sherman, John Adams never owned a slave, and he also was a member of the five-person committee that drafted the Declaration of Independence. Adams is widely credited as the primary author of Massachusetts's 1780 constitution. This constitution remains in effect, making it the oldest written constitution in the world. Article I of its bill of rights echoes the Declaration of Independence:

> All men are born free and equal, and have certain natural, essential, and unalienable rights; among which may be reckoned the right of enjoying and defending their lives and liberties; that of acquiring, possessing, and protecting property; in fine, that of seeking and obtaining their safety and happiness.[242]

In 1781, a slave named Quok Walker sued for his freedom. His attorney, Levi Lincoln, contended that slavery was "contrary to the Bible and the declaration of rights in the Massachusetts constitution."[243] The Supreme Court of Judicature ruled that Walker was a free man. Later cases affirmed the ruling, and by 1790, the state reported that it had no more slaves.[244]

John Quincy Adams was the first person to follow his father to the White House. After his defeat by Andrew Jackson in 1828, he returned to the House of Representatives, where he was a firm opponent of slavery. He is perhaps most famous for defending enslaved Africans who took over a ship named the *Amistad*. Joined by Roger Sherman's grandson, Roger Sherman Baldwin, he successfully argued for the slaves' freedom before the United States Supreme Court in 1841.[245]

On December 27, 1819, John Quincy Adams wrote to a friend that he eagerly awaited the day when "the seeds of the Declaration of Independence" would mature and slavery would meet its end.[246] The Declaration did not immediately end slavery, but it put it on the road to extinction—a very short road in the case of Massachusetts.

Why Did Slavery Continue?

Many founders opposed slavery for biblical and moral reasons, but there were other reasons for thinking that slavery, "in time, will not be a speck in our country."[247] In 1793, Noah Webster, already well known as an author of schoolbooks and later famous for his dictionary, published *Effects of Slavery on Moral and Industry*.[248] He had no doubt that "freedom is the sacred right of every man whatever be his color," but rather than rely on "abstract rights," this essay argued against slavery on the grounds of "private interest."[249] Drawing from world history and contemporary data, he contended that slavery simply is not an efficient or profitable institution. Among his arguments was that

> To labor solely for the benefit of other men, is repugnant to every principle of the human heart. Men will not be industrious, nor is it the will of heaven that they should be, without a well founded expectation of enjoying the fruits of their labor.[250]

Moreover, enslaved people had every incentive to steal from their "masters" and escape from captivity.

Webster, a member of the Connecticut Society for the Promotion of Freedom, was hardly an objective observer. His treatise was intended to give practical reasons for rejecting slavery to citizens who were not convinced that the institutional was unjust or unbiblical. The degree to which slavery was profitable in 1793 is debatable.[251] If it was unprofitable, especially in the North, that might help explain why Northern states adopted gradual manumission laws and many owners voluntarily manumitted their slaves. Unfortunately for enslaved Africans in the American South, a year after Webster published this treatise, another son of New England received a patent for a machine that gave slavery a new lease on life.[252]

Cotton producers had been using simple machines to separate cotton seeds from cotton fibers for centuries, but these machines only worked well for long-staple cotton. Eli Whitney's cotton gin was able to remove seeds from short-staple cotton, which made cotton production far more profitable. This, in turn, encouraged plantation owners to expand and increase production. Unfortunately, they turned to slave labor for these tasks.[253] The number of slaves in the American South increased dramatically in the early nineteenth century and so did support for slavery. By the 1820s, Southern leaders were arguing for the first time that slavery was a positive good.[254]

Conclusion

All humans are flawed. No serious student of the American founding should pretend that the founders—individually or collectively—were exempt from this reality. It is reasonable to criticize those founders who benefited from slavery, and it is certainly reasonable to wish that they would have banned this vile institution altogether. At the same time, we should also recognize that many founders never owned slaves, some of those who did freed them, and collectively, they took multiple steps that they believed would put slavery on the road to extinction. In addition, American Christians continued this fight in the nineteenth century. It is to this battle, and related ones, that we now turn.

CHAPTER FOUR

Evangelical Reformers in Antebellum America

Some progressives criticize Christians, especially evangelical Christians, for being conservative opponents of progress with respect to race. For instance, in a widely praised book, Jemar Tisby writes that "when faced with the choice between racism and equality, the American church has tended to practice a complicit Christianity...and in so doing created and maintained a status quo of injustice."[255] Similarly, Carolyn DuPont asserts that "[n]ot only did white Christians fail to fight *for* black equality, they often labored mightily *against* it" (emphasis original).[256] Of course, some Christians have opposed racial justice, but many have often been the leading advocates for freedom, justice, and equality in the United States.

America's founders did not create a thoroughly just utopia. Grave evils remained and were perpetuated in the new nation—most notably slavery and the unjust treatment of Native Americans. Many founders were concerned with these evils and worked to ameliorate or end them, but whatever successes they had, these and other problems persisted into the nineteenth century. In this chapter, I explore how Christians, often evangelical Christians, were on the forefront of battles to end slavery and protect Native Americans. My focus is on the antebellum era—that is, from the end of the War of 1812 until the start of the American Civil War.

Evangelicalism in the Nineteenth Century

Evangelicalism in the United States is usually dated to the First Great Awakening, a series of revivals throughout America in the 1730s. Virtually every American of European descent thought of himself or herself as a Christian in the eighteenth century, but these revivals caused some self-identified Christians to doubt their salvation, have conversion experiences, and join evangelical denominations. In the traditional telling of the tale, these revivals died down in the late eighteenth century and then blossomed again in the 1820s and 1830s in what is commonly referred to as the Second Great Awakening.

Scholars debate the extent to which these revivals waned in the eighteenth century and, if they did, when the Second Great Awakening began. However, there is widespread consensus that the 1820s and 1830s were marked by numerous revivals that encouraged Americans to repent of their sins, have conversion experiences, and join evangelical denominations. The most striking growth occurred among Methodists, who went from being 2.5 percent of the population in 1776 to 34.2 percent in 1850.[257] It was during this era that many Baptists shed their previously Calvinist views and became best characterized as evangelicals. By 1850, they constituted 20.5 percent of the American population.[258]

Today, we think of evangelicals as dominating the American South and being underrepresented in the North. In the early nineteenth century, the opposite was true. Evangelicalism was dominant in New England and was strong in the Mid-Atlantic and Western states. Evangelicals were well-represented in major metropolitan areas and among elites as well. It was not until the 1830s that evangelicalism swept the southern states and began to reshape the region into what is now sometimes called the Bible Belt.[259]

Who is an Evangelical?

The phrase "evangelical" has been used in a variety of ways, and there is no single accepted scholarly definition. Borrowing from the nineteenth-century minister Lyman Beecher, I consider evangelicals to be Protestants who adhere to historically orthodox Christian doctrines as articulated in the Apostles' Creed and who emphasize the need for a conversion experience, salvation by grace through faith in Christ alone, and the authority of the Bible as interpreted by individuals.[260] Evangelicals are committed to sharing the Gospel. Indeed, "evangelical" comes from the Greek word εὐαγγέλιον (euangelion), which means "good news." In antebellum America, approximately 33 percent of adult Americans are accurately labeled "evangelical" as opposed to 25 percent today.[261]

Before proceeding, it is necessary to briefly explore an important theological difference between nineteenth and twenty-first-century American evangelicals. With respect to eschatology (study of the end times), many contemporary evangelicals are premillennialists who believe that the world will become increasingly evil until Christ returns to rescue His people (I Thessalonians 4:17). Following this rescue, often referred to as the rapture, and a seven-year period of judgement known as the Tribulation, Christ will return to Earth, defeat the Anti-Christ and his allies, and reign on earth for one thousand years. After a final rebellion led by Satan, the Devil and those he deceives will be thrown in a "lake of fire," and Christ will reign over a new heaven and earth where "there shall be no more death, neither sorrow, nor crying, neither shall there be any more pain: for the former things are passed away" (Revelation 20–21; 21:4).

Some evangelicals in the early nineteenth century shared these views, but most were postmillennialists. They were convinced that God's Kingdom was already present and was advancing so forcefully that the "Gates of Hell" would not withstand it (Matthew 16:18). People from all nations would convert to Christianity, and Christians would work together to help end social evils. Eventually, Christ would return to usher in his Kingdom without a rapture, seven-year tribulation, or literal one-thousand-year reign.[262]

The political and social implications of these views are significant. Many nineteenth-century evangelicals believed that they could hasten Christ's return if they spread the Gospel and eliminated societal evils. Accordingly, they became energetic supporters of domestic and foreign missions. To help spread the Gospel they founded, among other organizations, the American Board of Commissioners for Foreign Missions (1810), the American Bible Society (1816), the American Sunday

School Union (1824), the American Tract Society (1825), and the American Home Mission Society (1826).

These evangelicals also formed literally thousands of organizations aimed at alleviating suffering and reforming society.[263] They were dedicated to benevolent activities such as feeding the poor, housing orphans, reforming prisons, fighting the abuse of liquor, aiding the mentally challenged, promoting peace, and educating the uneducated (including women and African Americans). Membership in these organizations often overlapped, and they were so prominent in antebellum America that they came to be referred to as the "Benevolent Empire."[264]

Women have always been central to the life of the Church, and in early America, they were sometimes able to influence politics indirectly through the advice they offered (e.g., Abigail Adams regularly shared her opinions with her husband) or publications (e.g., Mercy Otis Warren wrote under pseudonyms to support the patriot cause and, later, oppose the adoption of the proposed Constitution).[265] At the same time, they were almost always prohibited from voting and holding civic office. In antebellum America, women invented new ways to directly engage in political and social reform. They founded and led benevolent organizations, participated in political debates through essays, books, and public lectures, and lobbied legislators. Some of these women eventually joined what was then called the "woman movement" and advocated for social and political equality—especially the right to vote.[266] In this chapter, I highlight the roles Christian women played in opposing the evils of slavery and Indian removal. I do so because their contributions are often overlooked and because some of their strategies and tactics offer lessons for political engagement today.[267]

Christian Opposition to Slavery in Antebellum America

As we saw in the last chapter, virtually no founder defended slavery as a positive good and many were working actively to abolish it. Abolitionist societies flourished in the late eighteenth and early nineteenth centuries, and its leaders were committed to ending slavery *and* securing racial equality.[268] However, the invention of the cotton gin encouraged the expansion of slavery in the American South, and Southern leaders became increasingly defensive about the institution. After independence, most Southern evangelicals opposed slavery, but by 1830, many had come to support it. Indeed, the two most prominent evangelical denominations split over the issue: Methodists in 1844 and Baptists in 1845.[269]

Members of the Society of Friends, better known as Quakers, were among the earliest and most vocal opponents of slavery. In 1758, the Philadelphia Yearly Meeting formally condemned slavery, and in 1776 it agreed to disown Quakers who held slaves in its jurisdiction (Pennsylvania, New Jersey, and Delaware).[270] Friends remained among the most vocal critics of the institution in the nineteenth century. Among their greatest spokespersons were two sisters from South Carolina, Sarah and Angelina Grimké. The daughters of a prominent politician and slave owner from the state, Sarah moved to Philadelphia in 1821 and affiliated with the Quakers, and Angelina soon followed. Shortly thereafter, they became abolitionists.[271]

In 1835, Angelina joined the Philadelphia Female Anti-Slavery Society (founded and presided over by another Quaker, Lucretia Mott). In 1837, the Grimké sisters embarked on an antislavery lecture tour where they spoke at "at least eighty-eight meetings in sixty-seven towns" to more than 40,000 people.[272] At the time, it was considered inappropriate for women to address mixed audiences, but the sisters did so anyway. They also published numerous essays to promote the abolition of slavery, including Angelina's 1836 *Appeal to the Christian Women of the South* (1836), Sarah's *An Epistle to the Clergy of the Southern States* (1836), and Angelina's *An Appeal to the Women of the Nominally Free States: Issued by an Anti-Slavery Convention of American Women* (1837).

Members of the Society of Friends were important leaders in the abolitionist movement, but if only Quakers were abolitionists, the movement would never succeed. Even in Pennsylvania they were a minority, and they constituted only 0.003 percent of all Americans in 1855.[273] Fortunately for enslaved Americans, the far more numerous evangelicals soon became the hands and feet of the abolitionist movement.

Evangelical opposition to slavery can be traced back to the eighteenth century. English evangelicals, most notably William Wilberforce, led the fight to abolish the slave trade and slavery in the British Empire.[274] American evangelicals joined the battle as well. For instance, in 1790, the Baptist minister John Leland convinced the General Committee of Baptists to describe slavery as "a violent deprivation of the rights of nature, and inconsistent with a republican government" and to "recommend it to our brethren to make use of every legal measure, to extirpate the horrid evil from our land."[275] Although Quakers founded most of the early American abolitionists societies, they recognized that they needed allies if they were to abolish slavery throughout the nation. They welcomed evangelicals to join them, often placing them and other non-Friends in positions of leadership within these societies so that abolitionism would not be considered simply a Quaker idea.[276]

One of the most important evangelical opponents of slavery was the minister Charles Finney (1792–1879). He is best known as the evangelist who introduced new methods to revival meetings, such as holding protracted meetings that could last days, and the "anxious bench": a row of seats in the front of revival meetings where those especially convicted of sin could sit until moved to repent. In 1835, he became a professor of theology at the recently formed Oberlin College, and he became its president in 1850. Oberlin was one of the first colleges to admit African Americans on the same basis as whites and, in 1834, women—thus making it the nation's first coeducational college. Finney routinely denounced slavery, calling it a "great national sin," and refused communion to slaveholders. Under his leadership, Oberlin played an important role on the Underground Railroad.[277]

If Finney was one of the best-known male evangelists in the nineteenth century, Harriet Livermore (1788–1868) was among the best-known female evangelists. Raised a Congregationalist, she felt called to preach in 1821 and did so regularly in Free Will Baptist churches in New Hampshire. As her fame spread, she was invited to preach throughout the nation. In the early nineteenth century, church services were regularly held in the U. S. Capitol, and in 1827, she preached there to an overflowing audience (President John Quincy Adams had to sit on a stair because all seats were taken). She returned to preach in the Capitol in 1832, 1838, and 1848.

Livermore abhorred slavery. In 1829–1830, Virginia held a constitutional convention to draft a new constitution. She sent a letter and petition to former President James Madison, who was attending the convention as a delegate, urging him to ban the institution. She explained:

> I am a daughter of the happy part of our favored country called New England and of course an advocate for liberty. 2. I profess a belief in the gospel of Jesus Christ, & am consequently opposed to the Article of SLAVERY———3. I love my native country, therefore I am jealous of her laws, desiring they may be all equal, that no disproportion may offend the eye of Heaven, and draw divine judgments on a flourishing, enterprising, & (in some respects) happy Continent. 4. I feel myself in duty to my Savior, Master, & lawgiver, which is Christ Jesus, obligated to love my neighbor, [Matt. 22:39] especially to love the souls of men, women and children, for his Name sake, in whom there is all fulness of redemption, alike for Greek or Jew, barbarian Pythian bond or free, [Gal. 3:28] Glory, honor and praise for ever to his Great Name![278]

Like many evangelicals, Livermore drew direct lines between Christian liberty and the necessity of ending slavery. Alas, the letter and petition were not successful.

As might be expected, African Americans were committed abolitionists; the most famous of whom was Frederick Douglass (1818–1895). Born a slave in Maryland, he escaped to the North and became a leading abolitionist orator. He is best known for his autobiography *Narrative of the Life of Frederick Douglass, an American Slave* (1845). In his books and speeches, he provided compelling arguments not only against slavery but against the all-too-common belief that African Americans were inferior to whites. He joined the African Methodist Episcopal Zion Church, and in 1839, he became a licensed preacher.

Like Douglass, Isabella Baumfree (c. 1797–1883) was born into slavery. She escaped, and later sued successfully sued for the freedom of her son. In 1843, she became a Methodist, and on Pentecost Sunday of that year she changed her name to Sojourner because she was convinced that God was calling her to "travel up an' down the land, showin' the people their sins, an' bein' a sign unto them." She adopted "Truth" as a surname because she believed she was to "declare the truth to the people."[279] She traveled widely to camp meetings, where she displayed a white banner imprinted with the words "Proclaim liberty throughout all the land unto all the inhabitants thereof." Once she attracted a crowd, she would "tells 'em about Jesus, an' I tells 'em about the sins of this people.[280] In 1851, she delivered one of the most famous abolitionist speeches of the era, a speech which later became known by the title "Ar'n't I a Woman."[281]

Harriet Tubman (1822–1913) escaped from slavery in Maryland in 1849. As a young girl, she had been struck in the head by an iron weight and as a result suffered from migraines, seizures, and sleeping spells throughout her entire life. She nevertheless returned to the South a dozen times to help other slaves escape along a route known as the Underground Railroad, a network of African Americans and whites who helped slaves travel from slave states to free states or Canada.[282] She became known as the Moses of her people. Like Truth, she was a Methodist.[283]

Early abolitionists often advocated ending slavery gradually, but in the early 1830s, some abolitionists began to demand its immediate end. In 1831, William Lloyd Garrison started publishing his famous paper *The Liberator*, which aggressively advocated for the end of slavery. He and contributors to his paper had little patience with moderates, including Christian moderates. In the mid-1830s, Garrison and other radical abolitionists began to embrace highly unpopular views, including repudiating the United States Constitution, which Garrison called a "compact with the Devil."[284] Garrison and his followers may have begun as orthodox Christians, but their radical views led them away from both America's constitutional order and evangelicalism. Indeed, in 1858 the Garrisonian Wendell Phillips "denounced both George Washington and Jesus Christ as traitors to humanity, the one giving us the Constitution, the other, the New Testament."[285] Very few Americans agreed.

Far more representative of evangelical reformers who opposed slavery were Arthur and Lewis Tappan, wealthy New York businessmen who funded a wide range of missionary and reformist organizations (including the aforementioned Oberlin College). They helped found the American Anti-Slavery Society in 1833, and Arthur became its first president. The Tappans and their allies helped fund the printing and distribution of at least one million pieces of antislavery literature, and in 1837 the

Society organized antislavery petitions that were delivered to Congress. Within a year, more than 400,000 men and women had signed these petitions. By 1838, the Society had 1,300 local branches and 250,000 members.[286]

Catharine Beecher and Evangelical Criticism of Abolitionist Rhetoric

Some evangelicals opposed slavery, but feared that the aggressive tactics of abolitionist leaders were ineffective and dangerous. For instance, Catharine Beecher, the daughter of Lyman Beecher and sister of Harriet Beecher Stowe, criticized Angelina Grimké's vitriolic attacks on slave owners in *An Essay on Slavery and Abolition, with Reference to the Duty of American Females* (1837). She made it crystal clear that she opposed slavery, but argued that "character and measures" of abolitionist societies "are not either peaceful or Christian in tendency, but they rather are those which tend to generate party spirit, denunciation, recrimination, and angry passions."[287] Moreover, leaders like Garrison (whom she criticized by name), lack the Christian spirit of the great British abolitionists such as Wilberforce, Clarkson, Sharpe, and Macauley.[288] Beecher observed that some abolitionists defended such heavy-handed attacks by arguing that they are merely "preaching the truth and leaving the consequences to God,"[289] but this sort of rhetoric risks plunging the nation into a bloody "civil war," whose "train of fire would pass over us like a devouring fire."[290]

Beecher faulted the abolitionists not for their goals, but for the means they adopted to pursue them. Slavery would be ended through "persuasion," not "coercion." And benevolent women have a particularly important role to play in persuading slavery's supporters that the institution is evil and must be ended. Influenced by her eschatological views, she observed that slavery "is at no distant period to come to an end, is the unanimous opinion of all who either notice the tendencies of the age, or believe in the prophecies of the Bible."[291] The only question is the "time and manner of its extinction."[292] Beecher was confident that relying on persuasion would bring slavery's demise peacefully, whereas Grimkés' coercive approach would end in bloodshed.

Catharine Beecher

Catharine Beecher (1800–1878) was the first of Congregational minister Lyman Beecher's twelve children. A prominent advocate for the education of women, in 1823 she founded a school for women in Hartford, Connecticut, which historians contend was "one of the most significant advances made in early nineteenth-century education for women."[293] Among her pupils was her sister Harriett Beecher, who later taught at the school. Catharine later advocated for female education at the national level, through her involvement with the Central Committee for Promoting National Education (which she founded in 1843), the American Woman's Educational Association (begun in 1852), and the Milwaukee Female College (which she founded in 1850 and led until 1856). Beecher left behind a rich legacy of books, articles, and pamphlets including *The Elements of Mental and Moral Philosophy* (1831); *Letters on the Difficulties of Religion* (1836) and *Common Sense Applied to Religion* (1857). Her most influential book, *A Treatise on Domestic Economy for the Use of Young Ladies at Home and at School* (1841) went through more than fourteen editions. The work begins with extensive quotations from, and commentary on, Alexis de Tocqueville's magisterial *Democracy in America*. Of particular interest to Beecher was the critical role women play in the formation of good, republican citizens.

It is tempting to laud the radical abolitionists as righteous warriors, but Catharine Beecher's objections to their tactics may have lessons for our own day. Extremist rhetoric may be satisfying, but it results in political polarization. That is exactly what happened in antebellum America, and the result was a bloody civil war. It may be the case that Beecher was overly optimistic that slavery could be brought to peaceful end, but slavery *was* ended without bloodshed in the American North and mid-Atlantic states and in other countries. For instance, Brazil had 1.5 million slaves in 1874, but many were voluntarily manumitted before the country abolished the institution in 1888.[294]

Abolitionism after 1840

In 1840, the abolition movement split into irreconcilable factions. Its leaders disagreed about whether to pursue immediate abolition, the role of women in the movement, and whether it was best to rely on moral suasion or political action. One faction formed a political party, the Liberty Party, which was committed to the principle of abolishing slavery immediately. Unfortunately for enslaved Americans, very few of its members won political office.[295] The admission of Texas as a slave state in 1845 led to the formation of the Free Soil Party in 1848. The main goal of this party was to keep slavery from expanding beyond the current slave states. It nominated former president Martin Van Buren to be president in 1848, and he garnered 10 percent of the popular vote. The Fugitive Slave Act of 1850 stoked tensions dramatically as it provided incentives for Northern judges to declare African Americans brought before them by slave catchers to be slaves.

Inspired by the Fugitive Slave Act, Harriett Beecher Stowe wrote one of the most influential novels in America's history: *Uncle Tom's Cabin* (1852). The book sold more than 300,000 copies in its first year and reached the hearts and minds of many Americans.[296] Stowe convinced numerous Americans that slavery, even in its more humane manifestations, was a grave evil. In response to accusations that she misrepresented the "peculiar institution," in 1854 she published *A Key to Uncle Tom's Cabin*, which documented the horrors of slavery. When Abraham Lincoln met Stowe in 1862, he reportedly stated that she was "the little woman who wrote the book that started this great war."[297]

Bleeding Kansas and Beecher's Bibles

The Kansas-Nebraska Act of 1854 stipulated that the residents of each soon-to-be state would vote to permit or prohibit slavery. Advocates and opponents of slavery poured into the territories in hopes of influencing the outcome. A great deal of violence was committed by both sides, violence that included atrocities by the abolitionist John Brown (later famous for his 1859 raid on the federal arsenal in Harper's Ferry, Virginia). Henry Ward Beecher (1813–1887), yet another of Lyman Beecher's twelve children, played a role in this controversy. He was one of the most famous ministers of his day and a firm opponent of slavery. Beecher raised funds to buy rifles for the abolitionist forces in Kansas, observing that the weapons would be more valuable than "a hundred Bibles." Some of them were shipped in crates marked "books," and the press soon referred to them as "Beecher's Bibles."

In 1854, the Republican Party was created by former members of the Whig and Free Soil Parties. The new party formally opposed only the expansion of slavery, but many of its members were evangelical abolitionists. In 1860, the Republican nominee Abraham Lincoln was elected president without a single Southern electoral vote. Lincoln was no evangelical, but he was among the most theologically sophisticated of all presidents and, as we saw in the last chapter, he was committed to the principles of the Declaration of Independence.[298]

Historians, popular authors, and activists have spilled a great deal of ink debating what caused the Civil War, whether secession is constitutional, and Lincoln's commitment (or lack thereof) to abolitionism and racial equality. Regardless of where one comes down on these debates, there is no doubt that Lincoln's issuing of the Emancipation Proclamation on January 1, 1863 made ending slavery a central concern of the war. The Thirteenth Amendment, which was ratified on December 6, 1865, banned slavery and did much to help realize the majestic promises of the Declaration of Independence.[299]

The 1619 Project errs grossly by viewing the whole of American history through the lenses of slavery and racism. This account ignores the reality that by the founding era, many civic and religious leaders had come to understand that slavery was an evil that must be ended. In the nineteenth century, numerous citizens were motivated by the Christian convictions to work toward what they hoped would be its peaceful demise. We should not forget that slavery was ended peacefully in the American North and mid-Atlantic states, and Congress succeeded in prohibiting it from expanding into the upper mid-west. Many of these successes were due to the political activism of committed Christians.

Christian Opposition to Cherokee Indian Removal

Europeans came to the New World for many reasons, including religious liberty, economic profit, and missionary work. Many colonial charters and early laws spoke of the importance of converting Native Americans and bringing them the blessings of "civilization."

In the American southeast, colonists met with greatest success with five tribes that they referred to as the "Five Civilized Tribes." These were the Cherokee, Chickasaw, Choctaw, Creek (Muscogee), and Seminole. Of the five, the Cherokees had made the greatest progress by the 1820s—at least as defined by Western missionaries. Although each of these five tribes were eventually forced to move west of the Mississippi, in this section I focus on only the Cherokee Nation.[300] The removal of the Cherokee Indians from lands in Georgia, to which they clearly had a right, was the most controversial of all battles over Indian Removal.

A chief participant in these battles was Samuel Worcester, a missionary from the American Board of Commissioners for Foreign Missions (ABCFM) who lived among the Cherokee. Georgia authorities desired lands guaranteed to the Cherokee by federal treaties, and they viewed missionaries like Worcester as obstacles. Accordingly, the state passed a law banning white Americans from living on Cherokee land without a permit from Georgia. Worcester ignored the law, an act that resulted in an important Supreme Court decision that is discussed below.

In the 1820s, Georgia began pressuring the Cherokee Nation to exchange its land in Georgia for land west of the Mississippi. The Cherokees had no interest in this offer. The election of Andrew Jackson in 1828 stoked their fears that the United States would side with Georgia against the natives. To help plead their cause, the Cherokee legislature agreed to support publication of a newspaper; the *Cherokee Phoenix*. Samuel Worcester, with the aid of the ABCFM, secured a printing press for them. The first paper was printed on February 21, 1828 and contained news in both English and the Cherokee language. The paper was edited by a Native American who adopted the name Elias Boudinot after he met the founding president of the American Bible Society on his way to a school run by the ABCFM in Connecticut.[301]

The *Cherokee Phoenix* had influence well beyond the Cherokee Nation as Boudinot cleverly agreed to exchange copies of it with approximately a hundred other newspaper editors, some of whom then reprinted *Phoenix* articles. He regularly ran stories demonstrating the many ways the Cherokee had become "civilized." None of these reasons was as important to the many evangelicals who flocked to their support than the fact that many of them had become Christians.[302]

One of these evangelicals was Jeremiah Evarts (1781–1831), Secretary of the ABCFM and the person most responsible for securing a printing press for the Cherokees. Beginning on August 5, 1829, he published twenty-four essays defending the Cherokee cause under the pseudonym "William Penn," the founder of Pennsylvania who treated Native Americans with (relative) fairness and justice. He made a wide range of legal, political, and ethical arguments in support of Cherokee rights, and like many other reformers, he appealed to the spirit of the Declaration of Independence. He argued that how the United States treats the Cherokee will reveal whether or not the nation really believes that "*all men are created equal...[and] endowed by their Creator with certain inalienable rights.*"[303]

In the age of overlapping benevolent societies, it was no surprise that Jeremiah Evarts and Lyman Beecher were old friends. In 1829, Evarts met with Lyman's daughter Catharine and suggested, as she later recalled, that "American women might save these poor, oppressed natives and asked me to devise some method of intervention."[304] Her first step was to draft a circular letter entitled "To the Benevolent Ladies of the United States." Echoing arguments made by Evarts in his William Penn essays, to which she directed readers, she emphasized that the Cherokees "have a perfect *natural* right" to their lands and that "the government of the United States, by many treaties, have solemnly *promised* to protect them in their lawful possession of it (emphasis original)."[305] Unlike Evarts, she had to explain why women entered a political debate. She did so by referencing the biblical story of Esther, a woman who had been placed in a position of influence "for such a time as this" [Esther 4:14].[306]

Beecher then organized a meeting of prominent and influential evangelical women in her hometown of Hartford, Connecticut, where the letter was read and a plan was devised. These women, who included Lydia Sigourney, one of the most popular poets in the era, agreed to send the letter to prominent women in other towns, asking them to read and sign it. They then organized, circulated, and signed petitions that were sent to Congress on behalf of the Cherokee Indians. The circular was published and reprinted in multiple papers and collections, including the *Cherokee Phoenix*.[307] The response was overwhelming. Wilson Lumpkin, then serving as a member of the House of Representatives from Georgia, complained that Congress received "thousands" of petitions signed by "a million" men, women, and children. He was exaggerating, but by May of 1830, fifty-four petitions had been received by Congress, and two hundred would be received by the end of 1831.[308] As Steve Inskeep rightly observes, Beecher launched "the first mass political action by women in the history of the United States."[309]

Despite these petitions, Congress passed what became known as the Indian Removal Act in 1830, but the petitions must have been responsible for some of the ninety-seven votes against it in the House of Representatives (to the 102 votes in favor of it). The vote was largely along regional lines, with Southern representatives voting for the legislation (Davy Crockett, then serving as a representative from Tennessee, was a notable exception). Because of the Three-Fifths Compromise, the South had twenty "extra" representatives in House, sixteen of whom voted for removal. Without these extra votes, the removal bill would have failed.[310] The law empowered the president to provide Natives with land west of the Mississippi if they voluntarily gave up their lands in the east. Half a million dollars were appropriated to pay for their removal.

On March 13, 1831, members of the Georgia Guard arrested Worcester for violating the Georgia law prohibiting whites from living on Cherokee land. Worcester argued that the state had no authority over him, in part because he was a federal official (he had long served as a postmaster). The guard returned three weeks later with a letter from the state's governor informing him that he had been fired as postmaster, would receive no protection from the federal government, and warning him to leave. The guard returned a third time in July of 1831 and arrested Worcester. He was tried and convicted by a Georgia court and was sentenced to four years of hard labor.

Worcester's friends recognized that they could never win his case in state court, so they convinced former U.S. attorney general William Wirt to argue it before the United States Supreme Court. In *Worcester v. Georgia* (1831), the great Chief Justice John Marshall wrote that the Cherokee Nation had every right to the lands guaranteed to it by treaties with the United States and that Georgia had no right to regulate the Cherokee Nation or the people within it (including missionaries like Worcester) as a matter of state law.

Marshall's opinion was greeted with joy by Cherokee Indians and their allies and with virtual silence by Georgia and the president. Worcester remained in a Georgia jail, and the Georgia Guard continued to enforce state law on Cherokee lands. Andrew Jackson reportedly responded to the Court's decision with the comment, "Justice Marshall has made his decision; now let him enforce it."[311] There is no extant record of him saying these exact words, but his inaction spoke volumes. As Alexander Hamilton observed in Federalist 78, the Supreme Court has neither the power of the sword nor the power of the purse. The president simply refused to enforce the decision, and his allies continued to harass the Cherokees. Georgia freed Worcester in 1833, thus avoiding a final confrontation with the Supreme Court.[312]

After Jackson was reelected president in 1832, he determined to definitively solve the "Cherokee problem." In 1833, he offered the tribe $2.5 million for its land in Georgia—an offer that greatly exceeded earlier ones. Fatigued from years of battle and enticed by the offer, the tribe split into two factions: the National Party, which desired to stay, and the Treaty Party, which wanted to move west. In 1835, after a great deal of pressure, intimidation, and skullduggery, the Treaty Faction agreed to exchange Cherokee land in Georgia for western lands and $5 million. This figure was later raised to $6 million, but much of this money never made its way into Cherokee hands. The treaty was ratified by the Senate in 1836. It required the Cherokees to move west by March 28, 1836.[313]

Many Natives held out hope that the treaty would be modified or that they would at least gain extra time before they had to leave Georgia. After a series of miscommunications, General Winfield Scott began the evacuation of the Cherokees in March of 1836. He first forced them into camps, where disease ran rampant and killed as many as 2,000 Natives. The main migration began in the fall of that year, and preparations were so poor that another 600 Cherokees died.[314] Other scholars have estimated that as many as 4,000 to 8,000 Cherokees perished in what has aptly been named the Trail of Tears.[315]

Catharine Beecher observed in her circular letter that "if there is a Being who avenges the wrongs of the oppressed, [Indian removal is a cause] of alarm to our whole country."[316] My short account of the forced removal of the Cherokee from land guaranteed to them by treaties is just one of many such stories that must be remembered. At the same time, these stories are often told as if all white Americans and all government officials joined in oppressing Native Americans. As I have shown, many white Americans actively interceded on behalf of the Cherokee Nation, almost half of the members of the House of Representatives voted against Andrew Jackson's Indian policy, and the Supreme Court affirmed that they had a right to their land.

Evangelical Reform Movements as a Form of Social Control?

No student of nineteenth-century America denies that many Americans joined reform movements, but many scholars argue that they did because they were elites who desired to control others.[317] It is undoubtedly true that middle- and upper-class men and women were prominent in various reform organizations and that they wanted others to adopt their ideas. But attempting to influence or help people should not necessarily be equated with social control—at least in its invidious sense.

Many reform movements were not aimed at the "lower" classes. For instance, one of the earliest concerns of reformers was the elimination of dueling, something practiced almost exclusively by elites.[318] Likewise, opposition to alcohol was initially focused on the middle- and upper-class members of temperance societies who took pledges to avoid strong drink. Only later did the movement attempt to win converts among the "lower" classes and pursue a legal strategy of banning alcohol.[319]

Consider as well the two movements I explored in this chapter. As we have seen, many men and women sacrificed a great deal to bring slavery to an end. Some abolitionists were African American, so one could perhaps argue that they had an interest in ending slavery. Even if they had become free, there was always the threat that they might be unlawfully seized and enslaved after the Fugitive Slave Act of 1850. However, it is difficult to explain how *white* abolitionists were acting out of any sort of self-interest or desire to control others. The same is true for white evangelicals who opposed the unjust treatment of Cherokee Indians.

CHAPTER FIVE

The True Origins of the Separation of Church and State

Contrary to the assertions of some scholars, popular authors, and jurists, there is little evidence that America's founders desired to strictly separate church and state.[320] Thomas Jefferson and James Madison came close to embracing this ideal, but even these founders were not strict separationists when they served in public office. The vast majority of founders desired only to avoid a national established church, not to build a wall of separation between church and state.

A handful of early Americans, most notably Rhode Island's Roger Williams, embraced the separation of church and state for principled reasons. I presume contemporary advocates of this position, such as attorneys employed by Americans United for Separation of Church and State, do as well. Yet the story of how this doctrine became popular in the nineteenth century and persisted into the twentieth and twenty-first centuries is largely one of fear and hatred.

In certain respects, this chapter cuts against the major argument of this book as it involves some Protestants attempting to restrict the freedom of Catholics for what were, in part, religious reasons. Yet these Protestants were not acting out of pure anti-Catholic animus; they had reasons to distrust American Catholics. However, by the late twentieth century, changes in Catholic social and political thought enabled conservative Catholic and Protestant citizens to not only accept each other but also to work together on a host of important political matters.

This chapter serves as an important transition to the last two chapters. The idea that there should be a strict separation between church and state was primarily developed after the Civil War by Protestants to deny liberty and equality to Catholic citizens. In the mid-twentieth century, it morphed into a tool to be wielded against all religious citizens. For instance, it has been used to deny communities the freedom to celebrate religious holidays, memorialize fallen soldiers with monuments containing religious language or symbols, and engage in voluntary prayer. Separationists have also claimed that the First Amendment prohibits religious exemptions that protect religious minorities from general laws of neutral applicability (i.e., laws not targeting religious practices). But before we turn to these subjects, we need to understand how the pernicious idea that church and state must be strictly separated came into existence.

Nineteenth-Century Anti-Catholicism and the Blaine Amendments

Protestant suspicion of Roman Catholics is nothing new; some American colonies banned Catholics altogether, and many states did not permit them to hold civil office until the nineteenth century. Colonial laws prohibiting

Catholics were eventually repealed, often because of pressure from England. Support of the patriot cause during the War for American Independence and the aid Roman Catholic France encouraged many Protestants look more favorably on Catholic citizens, but anti-Catholic animus returned with a vengeance in the nineteenth century when the number of Catholics in the United States skyrocketed.[321] The following table charts Catholic growth as a percentage of the American population:

TABLE 1

1776:	1.8 percent
1850:	14 percent
1860:	21 percent
1890:	26 percent
1906:	32 percent
1926:	30 percent[322]

This growth was concerning to some Protestants because they considered the Catholic Church to be an evil, dangerous institution. This view was popularized by books such as *Awful Disclosures of Maria Monk, or, The Hidden Secrets of a Nun's Life in a Convent Exposed*, an 1836 "memoir" of former nun named Maria Monk that described in detail how priests would rape nuns and then baptize and murder their babies.[323] A slew of works of this nature, including *Six Months in a Convent* (1835), *The Testimony of an Escaped Novice* (1855), and *Rosamond: or, A Narrative of the Captivity and Sufferings of an Amer-*

ican Female under the Popish Priests, in the Island of Cuba (1834), were published in the mid-nineteenth century. Some of these books were loosely based on facts, but they were mostly figments of their authors' feverish imaginations.[324]

Other Protestants were concerned with the more realistic fear that Catholics could not be good republican citizens. For instance, Samuel Morse, the inventor of the telegraph, contended in a popular series of articles that were later published as *Imminent Dangers to the Free Institutions of the United States Through Foreign Immigration and the Present State of the Naturalization Laws* that "*Protestantism* favors *Republicanism*, while *Popery* as naturally supports *Monarchical* power" (emphasis in original).[325] Not only did Catholicism encourage political tyranny, but these immigrants are

> the priest-ridden troops of the Holy Alliance, with their Jesuit officers well skilled in all the areas of darkness. Now emigrants are selected for a service to their tyrants, and by their tyrants; not for their affinity to liberty, but for their mental servitude, and their docility in obeying the orders of their priests.[326]

Morse's solution to this problem was not to ban Catholic immigration altogether, but to pass a naturalization act that would prohibit all future immigrants from voting.[327] Similar books and pamphlets were published by Henry Ward Beecher, William C. Brownlee, Josiah Strong, and others.[328]

The fear that Catholicism was incompatible with republicanism and freedom was not completely unfounded. Throughout the nineteenth century, popes issued encyclicals and other formal proclamations—including *Mirari Vos* (1832), *Syllabus Errorum* (1864), *Immortale Dei* (1885), *Rerum Novarum* (1891), and *Testem Benevolentiae Nostrae* (1899)—which seemed to require the establishment of Roman Catholicism as the official state religion wherever possible and to condemn freedom of the press, democracy, and capitalism. Pope Pius IX even declared that "it is an error to believe that the Roman Pontiff can and ought to reconcile himself to, and agree with, progress, liberalism, and modern civilization."[329]

In 1870, the First Vatican Council embraced the heretofore contested doctrine of papal infallibility. This reinforced in many Protestant minds the concern that Catholics could not be independent and free citizens; they had to obey the pope's dictates. As the historian Michael Breidenbach has shown, in the eighteenth century, leading American Catholics had denied that the pope was infallible, but many nineteenth-century Catholic immigrants were ultramontanes who advocating supreme papal authority.[330]

Upon occasion, hatred of Catholics manifested itself in violence, such as when a Protestant mod burned down an Ursuline convent in Massachusetts in 1834. In this case, the angry mob was acting on an unfounded rumor that a Protestant woman was being held in the convent against her will.[331] A more civil response to the Catholic "threat" was the creation of public schools, a major purpose of which was to help form good, democratic, and Protestant citizens. Horace Mann of Massachusetts, sometimes called the father of the public school system, wrote that a nonsectarian public school earnestly inculcates all Christian morals; it founds its morals on the basis of religion; it welcomes the religion of the Bible; and, in receiving the Bible, it allows it to do what it is allowed by no other system – *to speak for itself* (emphasis in original).[332]

Mann had little doubt that this approach was non-sectarian, but to Roman Catholics, it was a very Protestant way of teaching religion. So, too, was the common practice of using the King James version of the Bible rather than the Douay version favored by Catholics. When Catholics objected to funding what they considered to be Protestant schools and asked for a share of state funds, or that the Douay Bible be read to their children, they were accused of being "sectarian." On more than one occasion, such requests were met with violence.

In 1842, Philadelphia's bishop asked that Catholic students be permitted to read from the Douay version of the Bible. To combat this perceived danger, the city's Protestant ministers formed the American Protestant Association. Conflicts between Catholics and Protestants became violent in 1844, and over the course of three days, Protestant rioters burned Catholic homes, a convent, and a church. At least fourteen people died. These riots, later known as the "Bible Riots," were among the most destructive, but they were far from the only examples of anti-Catholic violence.[333]

America's war with Roman Catholic Mexico (1846–1848) further inflamed anti-Catholic sentiments. The desertion of three hundred mostly Irish-American Catholic soldiers to the Mexican army did not help matters.

The Mexicans put them into their own unit, which became known as the "St. Patrick Battalion." Twenty-seven members of the battalion were executed for treason after the war. Ironically, to help retain Catholic soldiers, the United States Army appointed two Catholic priests to be army chaplains for the first time.[334]

In 1851, a Catholic priest in Maine was "tarred and feathered after he criticized a requirement that Catholics read from the Protestant Bible."[335] The following year, a political movement known as the Know-Nothings was formed. The movement earned its name because when members were asked about their political activities, they inevitably responded, "I know nothing." These activists were primarily motivated by anti-Catholic bigotry, and in the mid-1850s, they founded a political party known as the American Party. In 1854, about fifty-two of its members were elected to Congress, where they "pledged to oppose the pope and his minions."[336] Two years later, the party convinced former President Millard Fillmore to run under its banner. He received 23 percent of the popular vote.[337]

The American Party had run its course by 1860.[338] Among the critics of the party was the Republican Abraham Lincoln. In an August 24, 1855 letter to Joshua Speed, he wrote:

> I am not a Know-Nothing. That is certain. How could I be? How can anyone who abhors the oppression of negroes, be in favor of degrading classes of white people? Our progress in degeneracy appears to me to be pretty rapid. As a nation, we began by declaring that

"*all men are created equal.*" We now practically read it "all men are created equal, *except negroes.*" When the Know-Nothings get control, it will read "all men are created equals, except negroes, *and foreigners, and catholics.*" When it comes to that I should prefer emigrating to some country where they make no pretense of loving liberty—to Russia, for instance, where despotism can be taken pure, and without the base alloy of hypocrisy (emphasis original).[339]

When the American Party collapsed, its members who had been pro-slavery became Democrats, while those who were against slavery became Republicans. After the Civil War and Lincoln's assassination, the Republican Party adopted the American Party's anti-Catholicism. In an 1875 speech, President Ulysses S. Grant urged his audience:

Encourage free schools, and resolve that not one dollar, appropriated for the support of any sectarian schools. Resolve that neither the State nor Nation, nor both combined shall support institutions of learning...[that teach] sectarian, pagan, or atheistical dogmas. Leave the matter of religion to the family alter, the Church, and the private school, supported entirely by private contributions. Keep the Church and State forever separate.[340]

The speech was reprinted throughout the nation and was widely praised by Protestants. It was criticized by Catholics, who understood that it was—in the words of the *Catholic Standard*—"an attack on the Catholics of the United States."[341] Later that year, Grant asked Congress to pass a constitutional amendment requiring states to have public schools and prohibiting them from funding private ones. Representative James Blaine (R-Maine) obligated, proposing what has become known as the Blaine Amendment:

> No State shall make any law respecting an establishment of religion, or prohibiting the free exercise thereof; and no money raised by taxation in any State for the support of public schools, or derived from any public fund therefor, nor any public lands devoted thereto, shall ever be under the control of any religious sect; nor shall any money so raised or lands so devoted be divided between religious sects or denominations.[342]

Although neutral on its face, Columbia Law Professor Philip Hamburger argues persuasively that it was "an anti-Catholic measure that still permitted a generalized Protestantism in public schools."[343] It was deemed necessary because the First Amendment did not apply to the states and few states understood their constitutions to prohibit governments from funding "sectarian" schools.[344] The amendment passed overwhelmingly in the House but did not receive the necessary two-thirds vote in the Senate.

THE AMERICAN RIVER GANGES,

Thomas Nast, "The American River Ganges," *Harpers Weekly*, May 8, 1875

Thomas Nast was one of the most famous cartoonists in nineteenth-century America. Vehemently anti-Catholic, the above cartoon features bishop-like alligators from the Vatican attacking American school children. The "U.S. Public School" in the background has been demolished, and the American flag is flown upside down to signal distress. Above the ledge, lady liberty has been arrested and is being taken to the gallows.[345]

After the Blaine amendment failed, advocates sought to add similar amendments (often called "Baby Blaines") to state constitutions and "demanded that Congress require such clauses in the constitutions of territories seeking admission to the Union."[346] Eventually, between thirty-one and thirty-eight states adopted Blaine amendments (scholars and jurists debate whether some of these provisions are technically "Blaine amendments").[347] Although their supporters spoke broadly of "the sound principle of separation of church and state," their targets remained "sectarian" schools.[348] For instance, in New York, advocates emphasized that their amendment to separate church and state "cannot by any reasonable interpretation or construction be taken to prohibit the reading of the Bible in public schools."[349]

That "sectarian" in this context was a code word for "Catholic" has been recognized by seven Supreme Court justices to date. In *Mitchell v. Helms* (2000), Justice Thomas, writing for himself, Chief Justice Rehnquist, and Justices Scalia and Kennedy, observed:

> hostility to aid to pervasively sectarian schools has a shameful pedigree that we do not hesitate to disavow.... Opposition to aid to "sectarian" schools acquired prominence in the 1870's with Congress's consideration (and near passage) of the Blaine Amendment, which would have amended the Constitution to bar any aid to sectarian institutions. Consideration of the amendment arose at a time of pervasive hostility to the Catholic Church and to Catholics in general, and it was an open secret that "sectarian" was code for "Catholic".... Notwithstanding its history, of course, "sectarian" could, on its face, describe the school of any religious sect, but the Court eliminated this possibility of confusion when, in *Hunt v. McNair*, 413 U.S., at 743, it coined the term "pervasively sectarian"—a term which, at that

time, could be applied almost exclusively to Catholic parochial schools.[350]

This view is not limited to conservative justices. In the 2002 case of *Zelman v. Simmons-Harris*, Justice Steven Breyer, joined by Justices Stevens and Souter, noted that

> the "Protestant position" on this matter, scholars report, "was that public schools must be 'nonsectarian' (which was usually understood to allow Bible reading and other Protestant observances) and public money must not support 'sectarian' schools (which in practical terms meant Catholic)."…. And this sentiment played a significant role in creating a movement that sought to amend several state constitutions (often successfully), and to amend the United States Constitution (unsuccessfully) to make certain that government would not help pay for "sectarian" (*i.e.*, Catholic) schooling for children.[351]

For the first time, a majority of Americans embraced the idea that church and state should be strictly separated. Yet few actually believed in the abstract principle; they were primarily concerned with denying state funding for Roman Catholic schools.

Twentieth-Century Anti-Catholicism

Although Catholics were often viewed as a monolith by Protestants, there were in fact significant differences between Catholics from different ethnic groups. The First World War encouraged these groups to cooperate in new and significant ways. They began speaking with increased confidence in the debates of the time—for instance, in favor of censoring sexually explicit or sacrilegious movies. Protestant leaders often favored similar bans, but Catholic calls for censorship raised, in some minds, the specter of theocracy.[352]

The most infamous groups to respond to perceived Catholic threats in the 1920s and 1930s were the Fraternal Order of Masons and the reconstituted Ku Klux Klan.[353] The KKK is often thought of as a Southern phenomenon, but some of its largest chapters were in Indiana and Ohio. Klan-backed candidates were elected governor in Oregon, Colorado, Indiana, and Kansas.[354]

In 1922, the KKK and Masons helped convinced voters in Oregon to ban all private schools. Although the law was facially neutral, virtually all private schools in the state were Roman Catholic and—according to Hamburger—"secular and Protestant private schools received quiet assurances that they would be accommodated, leaving Catholics almost alone to challenge the law."[355] Fortunately, the United States Supreme Court declared Oregon's law to be unconstitutional in *Pierce v. Society of Sisters*, 268 U.S. 510 (1925).

The Democratic Party of the 1920s was hardly a bastion of toleration, but it was more friendly to Catholics than the Republican Party. In 1928, for the first time, a major party put a Roman Catholic on its presidential ticket. Alfred Emanuel Smith, an Irish Catholic and well-known opponent of Prohibition, had risen through the ranks of the Democratic Party and had been elected governor of New York four times. His political opponents charged that electing him as president would be tantamount to electing the pope. A well-known political cartoon entitled "Cabinet Meeting—If Al Were President" has the pope sitting at the head of a table surrounded by cardinals being served by Al Smith. The liquor bottle is labeled "nullification," which refers to Smith's desire to "nullify" the Nineteenth Amendment.

n.a. "Cabinet Meeting—If Al Were President." *The Fellowship Forum*, November 3, 1928[356]

Al Smith was, by some accounts, a lukewarm Catholic, and it is not clear that he was familiar with the Church's teachings on political and economic issues. When asked to defend papal encyclicals that seemed to be incompatible with American constitutionalism, he reportedly asked, "Will someone please tell me what the hell an encyclical is?"[357] Smith's faith may not have cost him the presidency, but it indisputably contributed to his losing the election to Herbert Hoover by 357 electoral votes.

The Second World War unified Americans in many ways, but Protestant-Catholic suspicions remained. Shortly after the war, the anti-Catholic polemicist Paul Blanshard began his meteoric rise to fame as a critic of Catholic power. In 1947 and 1948, he published a series of articles in *The Nation* describing how Catholicism and liberal democracy were incompatible. These articles became the basis for *American Freedom and Catholic Power*, which remained on the *New York Times* best-seller list of seven months.[358] Like Samuel Morse, he portrayed the pope as "the Commander-in-Chief of the Catholic army, and more than a million clerical soldiers throughout the world—priests, nuns, and brothers—follow him with unquestioning obedience."[359] Among his many complaints was that the Catholic Church was against "eugenic sterilization of certain insane, feeble-minded, and criminal citizens."[360] Blanshard published more than a dozen books criticizing Catholic power and was intimately involved with the creation of Protestants and Other Americans United for Separation of Church and State.

Coinciding with Blanshard's ascent, an organization with Nativist roots challenged a New Jersey program that reimbursed parents for the cost of transporting their children to parochial schools.[361] The group, the Junior Order of United American Mechanics, limited membership to "white, native-born Americans who were in 'favor of free education and opposed to any union of Church and State.'"[362] Among its goals was "to prevent sectarian interference [in public schools] and to uphold the reading of the Holy Bible therein."[363] The case resulted in the Supreme Court's case of *Everson v. Board of Education* (1947).

Hugo Black, author of the majority opinion in *Everson*, was a one-time member of the KKK.[364] His son later recalled:

> The Ku Klux Klan and Daddy, so far as I could tell, only had one thing in common. He suspected the Catholic Church. He used to read all of Paul Blanshard's books exposing power abuse in the Catholic Church. He thought the Pope and bishops had too much power and property.[365]

According to Hamburger, at least seven justices on the *Everson* court were members of "one Masonic organization or another" as well.[366]

The majority in *Everson* upheld a program that *benefited* families who sent their children to private schools, including Catholic schools, and anti-Catholic animus was not evident in either Black's or Rutledge's opinions. The same cannot be said about Justice Jackson's dissenting opinion (which was joined by Rutledge). Jackson observed that the Catholic Church "relies on early and indelible indoctrination in the faith and order of the Church by the word and example of persons concentrated to the task. Our public school, if not a product of Protestantism, at least is more consistent with it than with the Catholic culture and scheme of values."[367]

Eleven days after *Everson* was decided, Senator Robert Taft introduced a federal education bill that would have provided grants to states, which could in turn distribute funds to public and private schools—including religious ones. The possibility of federal funds making their way to religious (especially Catholic) schools led James M. Dawson, director of the Baptist Joint Committee, to call a "meeting of Protestant, educational, and fraternal leaders."[368] These individuals founded Protestants and Other Americans United for Separation of Church and State in 1948. The organization's founding manifesto complained of a "powerful church, unaccustomed in its own history and tradition to the American ideal of separation of church and state."[369] Catholics could be excused for thinking that the organization was targeting them.

Separationist Rhetoric Becomes a Reality: And Catholics *and* Protestants Join Forces to Oppose it

The logic of both the majority and dissenting opinions in *Everson* pointed toward the strict separation of church and state, a direction confirmed by the Court's decision in *McCollum v. Board of Education*, (1948).[370] Here, by an eight-to-one vote, justices invalidated an Illinois plan that set aside part of a school day for voluntary religious instruction. Many traditional Protestants were stunned by the opinion. In Hamburger's words:

> They had sought their familiar Prot-
> estant separation and now suddenly

found themselves confronted with a
secular version, which threatened the
nonsectarian religiosity of America's
institutions.[371]

A few years later, justices seemed to take a step back
in *Zorach v. Clauson*, 343 U.S. 306 (1952) when they upheld
a plan that permitted students to be released from school
early to receive religious instruction.

The Supreme Court refrained from deciding additional religion clause cases in the 1950s, but passionate
debates about church-state relations continued.
Anti-Catholicism subsided significantly in the late
1950s and 1960s, in part because of the Catholic
Church's longtime stand against the evils of commu-
nism. As well, Catholic authors and media personalities such as Thomas Merton and Bishop Fulton J. Sheen
attracted a significant Protestant following. Merton's
Seven Story Mountain "presented Catholic spirituality
in an appealing and non-threatening light."[372] Sheen's
highly popular television show *Life Is Worth Living* was
watched by 30 million viewers at its peak. He offered
viewers moral and religious lessons that appealed to
Catholics and Protestants alike.[373]

As might be expected, members of Protestants
and Other Americans United vigorously opposed the
nomination and election of John F. Kennedy. Candidate Kennedy's proclamation that "I do not speak for
my church on public matters—and the church does
not speak for me" helped to calm Protestant anxiet-
ies.[374] After winning a close election against Richard
Nixon, the young, handsome president and his beautiful family won the hearts of the American people. He

remains among the most popular of all U.S. presidents and indisputably helped many Protestants understand that Catholics can be loyal citizens.[375]

In 1961, Pope John XXIII called for a council of Roman Catholic bishops and cardinals from throughout the world. Known as the Second Vatican Council, Catholic leaders met from 1962 to 1965 and made sweeping changes to the church. Most critically for our purposes, the Catholic church clearly and officially embraced democracy and individual liberty, including religious liberty. The mass, which had heretofore been in Latin, would now primarily be performed in local languages, and Protestants were declared to be fellow Christians. Between 1974 and 1990, thirty formerly authoritarian countries, many of which were Catholic, became democracies. It seemed, at least to Protestant observers, that the Catholic church had finally embraced democracy and liberty.[376]

Just as Protestant suspicions of Catholics were abating, the Supreme Court issued a decision that appeared to many to be anti-religious.[377] In *Engel v. Vitale*, 370 U.S. 421 (1962), justices ruled six to one that teacher-led prayer in public schools was unconstitutional. The decision was widely denounced by Protestant and Catholic groups alike. Not to be deterred, the following year the Court ruled eight to one against Bible reading and recitation of the Lord's Prayer in public schools.[378] These decisions were opposed by 70 percent of the American public and forty-nine of the nation's governors. Members of Congress proposed 146 separate constitutional amendments to overturn them.[379]

Without doubt, some Americans have favored the separation of church and state as a matter of principle. However, as we have seen, the doctrine was never popular until it was connected to anti-Catholicism, and the vast majority of Americans repudiated it as soon as they perceived it as being anti-religious. Simply put, many Protestants supported separationism because they understood it to limit Catholic power; they never imagined that the doctrine would ban or restrict practices favored by them.[380] When the Supreme Court started using the Establishment Clause to declare that practices such as school prayer were unconstitutional, they rejected separationism.

Protestants and Catholics Together

In the 1960s, traditional Protestants and Catholics came together to oppose what they considered to be the forces of secularization. After years of opposing governmental aid to religious schools, Protestants joined Catholics in supporting the Elementary and Secondary Education Act of 1965, which provided funding to public and private schools. The vast majority of private schools were, and are, religious schools. Protestants and Catholics were soon cooperating on a host of issues.

Throughout this section, when I refer to Protestants and Catholics, I mean *traditional* Protestants and Catholics. Traditional believers adhere to the historical doctrines associated with each tradition, and they practice their faiths (i.e., they go to church, pray, and so forth). There are, of course, nominal or progressive Protestants and Catholics who differ from their coreligionists on the social and political issues discussed below.

Measuring Religion

Social scientists have developed scales to measure the sort of distinction I am making between conservative and progressive Protestants and Catholics. For instance, the political scientist James Guth and colleagues distinguish between traditionalists—who "adhere to orthodox beliefs, participate frequently in normative religious behaviors, and want their religious institutions to adhere to traditional beliefs and practices"—and modernists—who reject orthodox beliefs, do not regularly participate in religious activities, and want their religious institutions to change. These differences lead to strikingly different political decisions. The 2004 presidential election featured the Protestant George Bush running against the Catholic John Kerry. At first glance, Bush narrowly won the Catholic vote: 53 percent to 47 percent. However, a closer look shows that Bush won 81 percent of the white traditional Catholic vote, but only 27 percent of the white modernist Catholic vote.[381]

In 1971, the Southern Baptist Convention passed a resolution supporting a woman's right to have an abortion for a host of reasons. It reaffirmed this position in 1974. Protestants, generally, were not troubled by abortion in the early 1970s. Opposition to the practice was led primarily by Roman Catholics, who were convinced for theological reasons that human life begins at conception. When the Supreme Court declared state laws prohibiting abortion to be unconstitutional in *Roe v. Wade* (1973), the number of abortions skyrocketed from 750,000 in 1973 to 1.5 million in 1980.[382] During these years, Protestants became increasingly opposed to the practice.

Shortly after *Roe*, the influential evangelical magazine *Christianity Today* printed an editorial decrying the decision. The following year, the prominent pediatric surgeon C. Everett Koop published a pro-life treatise *The Right to Live; the Right to Die*. A few years later, Koop teamed up with the evangelical theologian Francis Schaeffer to produce a movie entitled "What Ever Happened to the Human Race?" By the 1980 presidential election, traditionalist Protestants were thoroughly pro-life.

The moral chaos of the late 1960s and early 1970s drew Protestants and Catholics together to cooperate on a variety of causes, none more important than advocating for the protection of unborn babies. Collectively, they protested at abortion clinics and worked to elect pro-life politicians who might one day pass a constitutional amendment to repudiate *Roe* or appoint and confirm justices who would overturn the decision. When such attempts failed, they attempted to limit access to abortion and to encourage women to choose life by supporting crisis pregnancy centers and similar organizations.[383]

In 1994, evangelical and Catholic leaders issued an important declaration entitled "Evangelicals and Catholics Together: The Christian Mission in the Third Millennium." The declaration was particularly significant because evangelicals have been more prone to anti-Catholicism than, say, Lutherans or Anglicans. The document outlined major areas of agreement on theological matters, acknowledged some areas of disagreement, but emphasized the necessity of "cooperating as citizens" on political issues such as abortion, pornography, euthanasia, and religious liberty.[384] Of course, Catholics and Protestants still have theological disagreements, and sometimes they have political ones as well, but the day has long passed when Protestants did not believe Catholics could be good citizens.

Conclusion

We should rejoice that Protestants and Catholics have joined forces to advocate for political goals such as protecting unborn life and supporting religious liberty. Unfortunately, the idea that church and state should be strictly separated remains powerful in American culture. Groups such as Americans United for Separation of Church and State, Freedom From Religion Foundation, and American Humanist Association regularly argue that the First Amendment requires such separation. Among the practical implications of this doctrine is that the public square must be stripped of religious language and images. It is to this issue that we now turn.

CHAPTER SIX

Must Religion be Stripped from the Public Square?

In 2012, Ohio approved a Holocaust and Liberators Memorial, a central feature of which is a fractured Star of David.[385] Before it was dedicated, the Freedom From Religion Foundation sent a letter to head of the State's Holocaust Memorial Committee objecting to erecting a "religious symbol on government property."[386] The organization had no objection to the memorial per se, merely the inclusion of a "readily identifiable Jewish symbol."[387] Attorneys from the Freedom From Religion Foundation argued that the First Amendment prohibits religious symbols on public property.

There is little doubt that the Star of David is a religious symbol. In the nineteenth century, it became widely accepted by European Jews as "a striking symbol that would represent Judaism as the cross did Christianity."[388] The State of Israel embraced it as well; indeed, it is featured on Israel's flag. It is also the central symbol in the Magen David Adom or "Red Shield of David"— Israel's equivalent of the Red Cross.[389] It is often featured prominently on or in Jewish synagogues.

Ohio Holocaust Memorial

The Freedom From Religion Foundation, Americans United for Separation of Church and State, and the American Humanist Association regularly argue that religious symbols on public property violate the First Amendment's Establishment Clause ("Congress shall make no law respecting an establishment of religion..."). They have made this claim with respect to holiday displays such as manger scenes and menorahs, World-War-One-era memorial crosses, and monuments of the Ten Commandments. These and related organizations have also challenged the use of the words "under God" in the Pledge of Allegiance and "In God We Trust" on American currency. They have also objected to state legislatures and city councils beginning their meetings with prayer.

We often think about the freedom of *individuals* to engage in religious activity, but we must recognize that *communities* should be free to engage in religious speech, recognize the existence of God, and celebrate religious holidays. To deny their ability to do so infringes upon their religious liberty. The First Amendment in no way requires the removal of religious symbols, imagery, and language from the public square.

In the 1947 case of *Everson v. Board of Education*, Justice Wiley Rutledge argued "[n]o provision of the Constitution is more closely tied to or given content by its generating history than the religious clause of the First Amendment. It is at once the refined product and the terse summation of that history."[390] Rutledge penned a dissenting opinion, but the majority opinion by Justice Hugo Black agreed that the Establishment Clause of the First Amendment must be interpreted in light of its "generating history."

With respect to the Establishment Clause, justices make two sorts of historical arguments. The first looks to the founding era to determine what America's civic leaders, specifically the men who drafted and ratified the First Amendment, understood it to mean.[391] There is a great deal of evidence that America's founders did not desire the strict separation of church and state.[392] Indeed, there was widespread agreement that governments at all levels could support, encourage, and promote Christianity and Christian ideas. There is no question that an originalist understanding of the First Amendment permits practices that are objected to by groups such as the Freedom From Religion Foundation. I will not rehearse these arguments here, but encourage readers interested in them to read Chapters Three and Four of *Did America Have a Christian Founding?*

In this chapter, I explore another historical argument that United States Supreme Court justices have made to support the constitutionality of religious monuments and speech on public land, or by public officials. In addition to looking at the founders' understanding of the religion clauses, they have considered whether a particular practice has deep roots in our country's history. That is, have local, state, and national governments regularly permitted religious images and language on public property? The answer is a resounding "yes."

Historical Practices Since the Founding Era

Let's begin by considering the constitutionality of that most religious of all practices: prayer. In the case of *Marsh v. Chambers* (1983), justices considered whether Nebraska could pay a legislative chaplain and open its sessions with prayer.[393] Chief Justice Warren Burger, for the Court, held that these practices did not violate the Establishment Clause. Central to his opinion was the fact that the men who drafted and approved the First Amendment agreed to hire legislative chaplains and approved of legislative prayer,[394] but he went beyond the founding era to observe that the nation and states have had a long tradition of engaging in these practices: one that stretches from the founding era to the present day. As such, they are "deeply embedded in the history and tradition of this country" and are therefore constitutional.[395]

More recently, in *Town of Greece v. Galloway*, justices considered the constitutionality of a city council's practice of opening its meetings with prayer.[396] In his majority opinion, Justice Anthony Kennedy observed that the "Court's inquiry, then, must be to determine whether the prayer practice in the town of Greece fits within the tradition long followed in Congress and the state legislatures."[397] Drawing heavily from founding era practices and practices since that time, he concluded that opening a city council meeting with prayer is constitutional.

Concurring opinions in *Greece v. Galloway* by Justices Samuel Alito and Clarence Thomas, like Justice Elena Kagan's dissenting opinion, all made historical arguments to support their respective conclusions. It is noteworthy that Justice Kagan specifically noted that she agreed with the majority that the issue is "whether the prayer practice in the Town of Greece fits within the tradition long followed in Congress and the state legislatures."[398] She, along with Justices Ginsburg, Breyer, and Sotomayor, interpreted this history differently than the majority, but it bears emphasizing that no justice rejected the proposition that history plays a critical role in helping justices resolve such cases.[399]

What about religious displays on public property? In *Lynch v. Donnelly*, Chief Justice Burger wrote for a majority of the justices that a nativity scene on public property was constitutional. Chief among his reasons was that "[t]here is an unbroken history of official acknowledgement by all three branches of government of the role of religion in American life from at least 1789."[400]

In the 1989 case of *County of Allegheny v. ACLU*, Justice Blackmun's majority opinion found one holiday display on public property to be constitutional and another to be unconstitutional.[401] In an opinion concurring in part and dissenting in part, Justice Anthony Kennedy observed that:

> Our cases disclose two limiting principles: government may not coerce anyone to support or participate in any religion or its exercise; and it may not, in the guise of avoiding hostility or callous indifference, give direct benefits to religion in such a degree that it, in fact, "establishes a [state] religion or religious faith, or tends to do so."[402]

With respect to religious displays on public property, he concluded that:

> [T]he principles of the Establishment Clause and our Nation's historic traditions of diversity and pluralism allow communities to make reasonable judgments respecting the accommodation or acknowledgement of holidays with both cultural and religious aspects. No constitutional violation occurs when they do so by displaying a symbol of the holiday's religious origins.[403]

Kennedy was exactly right: communities are free to celebrate religious holidays. Such celebrations are "deeply embedded in the history and tradition of this country" and are therefore constitutionally protected.[404]

In recent years, there have been a number of cases concerning the constitutionality of crosses, monuments of the Ten Commandments, and religious language on public property. I am currently serving as an expert witness for the State of Arkansas in a lawsuit challenging the constitutionality of a monument of the Ten Commandments on the State House Grounds. Among my duties was to write a report demonstrating that the nation and states have a long tradition of erecting religious symbols and using religious language on public grounds. The trial has not yet occurred, but hopefully the decision based on the evidence presented below will forever put to rest the idea that religion must be expelled from the public square.

Crosses

The cross is perhaps the best known symbol of Christianity. Christians regularly display and wear crosses in remembrance of Jesus Christ's sacrifice for humanity. Throughout American history, crosses have often been used to commemorate and honor the dead. In the context of war, they are regularly used to recognize the sacrifice that soldiers have made for their nation.[405] Most notably, hundreds of thousands of tombstones with crosses on them fill Arlington National Cemetery and the other 143 National cemeteries throughout the Nation.[406] Other crosses on public land include[407]:

- In Richmond, Virginia, a large Latin cross set near the falls of the James River. Known as the

Christopher Newport Cross, it commemorates the 1607 expedition of Captain Newport, who sailed upriver as far as the falls, and bears the inscription 'Dei Gratia Virginia Condita,' or 'Virginia was founded by the Grace of God.'

- In Mobile, Alabama, a large stone cross, known as the Bienville Cross, sits in the heart of downtown in a public square. As shown by its inscription, it is a monument to Jean Baptiste LeMoyne, Sieur de Bienville (1680-1768), founder of the city, whose recited accomplishments include bringing 'the Prosperity of true Civilization and the Happiness of real Christianity.'

- The Father Millet Cross, which currently stands in Fort Niagara State Park in upstate New York, was originally erected in 1688 by a Jesuit priest, Father Pierre Millet. In 1925, President Calvin Coolidge set aside a 320-square-foot section of Fort Niagara Military Reservation 'for the erection of another cross commemorative of the cross erected and blessed by Father Millet.'

- In Santa Fe, New Mexico, there is the Cross of the Martyrs, a large steel cross erected to commemorate the 21 Franciscan Friars who perished in the 1680 Indian uprising known as the Pueblo Revolt.

- The Cross Mountain Cross, in Fredericksburg, Texas, stands where the first settlers of what is now Fredericksburg first discovered a timber cross on a hilltop in 1847. A cross has remained there since; the original replaced with a permanent lighted version in 1946, which today resides in the city-maintained Cross Mountain Park.

- Since 1858, a cross has stood atop the Chapel of the Centurion at Fort Monroe, in Hampton, Virginia. Named for Cornelius, the Roman centurion converted to Christianity by St. Peter, the Chapel served as the United States Army's oldest wooden structure in continuous use for religious services until it was decommissioned in 2011.

- The Irish Brigade Monument, a 19-foot Celtic cross, was placed in Gettysburg National Military Park in 1888 to honor soldiers from three New York regiments who fought and died at Gettysburg.

- The Jeannette Monument at the United States Naval Academy, a Latin cross dedicated to sailors who died exploring the Arctic in 1881, was erected in 1890 and is the largest monument in the Naval Academy Cemetery.

- The Father Serra Cross is an 11-foot granite Celtic cross donated to the City of Monterey in 1905 and installed on public land in 1908. The cross features a portrait of Father Junipero Serra and an image of his Carmel Mission.

- A large Celtic cross known as the Wayside Cross sits in New Canaan, Connecticut's historic green. Erected in 1923 as a war memorial, it bears the inscription: 'Dedicated to the glory of Almighty God in memory of the New Canaan men and women who, by their unselfish patriotism, have advanced the American ideals of liberty and the brotherhood of man.'

• Then, in New York City, there stands the Ground Zero Cross. Composed of steel beams approximating the shape of a Latin cross and found amid the wreckage of the World Trade Center, the cross is now erected at the National September 11 Memorial & Museum.

In 1919, a group of private citizens formed a committee to memorialize the young men from Prince George's County, Maryland, who died in the First World War. When the committee ran out of money, the local American Legion took over the project and erected a 32-foot-high Latin cross made of concrete. Completed in 1925, the cross, often referred to as the Bladensburg Cross, was originally on private land, but as the area around the cross was developed, the monument was surrounded by busy roads. In 1961, Maryland acquired the land and agreed to maintain the cross, but the American Legion retained the right to use the site for ceremonies. In 2014, the American Humanist Association filed suit in a federal district court and argued that the memorial violated the First Amendment's Establishment Clause and must be removed or destroyed.[408]

The Bladensburg Cross (Courtesy of DB King)

In *American Legion v. American Humanist Association* (2019), the Supreme Court ruled seven to two that having such a memorial on public land is constitutionally permissible. Justice Samuel Alito, in his majority opinion, noted that justices often look "history for guidance" when deciding such cases.[409] He concluded that where "categories of monuments, symbols, and practices with a longstanding history follow in that tradition, they are likewise constitutional."[410] The Bladensburg Cross fits this category.[411]

Justices Ruth Bader Ginsburg and Sonia Sotomayor dissented from the Court's ruling, but not its use
of history. Indeed, Ginsburg referenced three different
founders and founding documents to buttress her opinion.[412] Although relying on history is associated with
conservative rather than liberal justices, in Establishment Clause cases, liberals are actually slightly more
likely to make historical arguments than are conservatives.[413] Unfortunately, most of their historical arguments
are simply wrong.

In the late eighteenth century, approximately 98
percent of Americans of European descent were Protestants, 2 percent were Roman Catholics, and there were
approximately 2,000 Jews in a handful of American
cities.[414] The number of Catholics and Jews increased
dramatically in the nineteenth and early twentieth
centuries, but more than 90 percent of all citizens still
identified themselves as Christians well into the twentieth century.[415] Each of the young men from Saint
George's county identified themselves as Christians,
and the Latin cross was regularly used to memorialize
the men who sacrificed their lives in that war. The Court
properly concluded that given these facts, and the long
history of memorializing soldiers with crosses, there was
nothing constitutionally problematic about the Bladensburg Cross.

Today, however, America is a far more diverse country.
Approximately 64 percent of Americans continue to
identify themselves as Christians, but 6 percent are
adherents to non-Christian faiths, and 30 percent associate themselves with no faith at all.[416] It would thus be
inappropriate to memorialize Americans who sacrificed
their lives in, say, Afghanistan and Iraq, with a single

religious symbol. Communities should be inclusive in their memorials, perhaps by utilizing different religious symbols.

Before the First World War, soldiers buried in national cemeteries had tombstones featuring Latin crosses. After the war, the military permitted the tombstones of Jewish soldiers to include the Star of David.[417] Today, tombstones may feature one of seventy-five symbols, including the Crescent and Star for Muslims, a Nine-Pointed Star for members of the Baha'i faith, and even a symbol for atheists.[418] Similarly, the 9/11 Memorial in New York City contains multiple religious images. This is entirely appropriate, as it may well cause offence to memorialize people with symbols taken from faiths to which they do not adhere. Of course, some religious images are accepted by multiple faiths and even by citizens who have no faith at all. It is to such a symbol that we now turn.

Ten Commandments

Crosses are often associated with Christianity, but the Ten Commandments are accepted by Jews, Christians, and Muslims. The commandments are numbered and listed in different ways by various faith traditions, but Jewish and Christian lists are substantially the same.[419] Even in the context of a religious building such as a church or synagogue, a display of the Ten Commandments is arguably not *simply* religious, as some of the commandments—such as "do not kill"—are moral precepts shared by people of different faiths and no faith at all.

In the mid-twentieth century, E.J. Ruegemer, a Minnesota judge, became concerned with the rise of juvenile delinquency in the United States. He believed that "if troubled youths were exposed to one of mankind's earliest and long-lasting codes of conduct, those youths might be less inclined to break the law."[420] He formed a committee "consisting of fellow judges, lawyers, various city officials, and clergy of several faiths" to develop a "version of the Ten Commandments which was not identifiable to any particular religious group."[421] He eventually partnered with Cecil B. DeMille and the Fraternal Order of Eagles to help place granite monuments inscribed with the Ten Commandments throughout the United States.[422] Many of these monuments were placed on public property, in one case on the Texas State House grounds. Not surprisingly, separationist groups have raised multiple challenges to such monuments.[423]

The United States Supreme Court considered the constitutionality of displaying the Ten Commandments on public property in two cases decided on the same day: *Van Orden v. Perry*,[424] and *McCreary County v. ACLU of Kentucky*.[425] In *Van Orden*, five justices agreed that a granite monument commemorating the Ten Commandments on the Texas State House grounds did not violate the Establishment Clause. However, in *McCreary*, five justices declared paper copies of the Ten Commandments posted in a county courthouse to be unconstitutional. Although these rulings may appear to be contradictory, four justices believed both displays were unconstitutional and four thought both were constitutional. Justice Breyer cast the deciding vote in both cases.

These two cases generated ten opinions, historical arguments and the context of the displays playing an important role in both cases.[426] In these cases and elsewhere, Justice Breyer appeared to adopt a rule that older monuments are constitutional but new ones are not. As I argue below, this is an imprudent rule that would discriminate against non-Christian faiths. Fortunately, since these two cases, the composition of the Supreme Court has shifted significantly; a majority of justices are now committed to interpreting the Establishment Clause in light of the founders' views and longstanding practices. There is little danger of the current Court concluding that religion must be stripped from the public square.

In *Van Orden v. Perry*, Chief Justice William Rehnquist observed that "acknowledgements of the role played by the Ten Commandments in our Nation's heritage are common throughout America."[427] To illustrate this point, he noted:

> We need only look within our own Courtroom. Since 1935, Moses has stood, holding two tablets that reveal portions of the Ten Commandments written in Hebrew, among other lawgivers in the south frieze. Representations of the Ten Commandments adorn the metal gates lining the north and south sides of the Courtroom as well as the doors leading into the Courtroom. Moses also sits on the exterior east facade of the building holding the Ten Commandments tablets.
>
> Similar acknowledgments can be seen throughout a visitor's tour of our Nation's Capital. For example, a large statue of Moses holding the Ten Command-

ments, alongside a statue of the Apostle Paul, has overlooked the rotunda of the Library of Congress' Jefferson Building since 1897. And the Jefferson Building's Great Reading Room contains a sculpture of a woman beside the Ten Commandments with a quote above her from the Old Testament (Micah 6:8). A medallion with two tablets depicting the Ten Commandments decorates the floor of the National Archives. Inside the Department of Justice, a statue entitled "The Spirit of Law" has two tablets representing the Ten Commandments lying at its feet. In front of the Ronald Reagan Building is another sculpture that includes a depiction of the Ten Commandments. So too a 24-foot-tall sculpture, depicting, among other things, the Ten Commandments and a cross, stands outside the federal courthouse that houses both the Court of Appeals and the District Court for the District of Columbia. Moses is also prominently featured in the Chamber of the United States House of Representatives.[428]

As an expert witness for the State of Arkansas, I was asked to testify as to whether erecting monuments of the Ten Commandments is a practice that is "deeply embedded in the history and tradition of this country."[429] I was able to track down a total of 106 of these monuments inspired by the Fraternal Order of Eagles on public land, all of which were erected between 1956 and 1983.[430]

Massive granite monuments of the Ten Commandments are perhaps the most conspicuous displays of the Ten Commandments, but many other representations of them exist, including:

a. a plaque containing the full text of the Ten Commandments in Alabama's State Capitol,[431]

b. a framed copy of the Commandments in Georgia's State Capitol,[432]

c. a mural of Moses with the Ten Commandments in the Rumford District Court courtroom in Rumford, Maine,[433]

d. a mural of Moses receiving the Ten Commandments in the Capitol Courtroom in Saint Paul, Minnesota,[434]

e. a mural of Moses holding the Ten Commandments in the Queens Supreme Court Building, New York,[435]

f. a mural of Moses carving the Ten Commandments in the State Supreme Court building in Harrisburg, Pennsylvania, and[436]

g. a mural of Moses holding the Ten Commandments in the Supreme Court Room, City-County Building, Pittsburg, Pennsylvania.[437]

Ten Commandments Monument, Arkansas Statehouse Grounds

There is little doubt that erecting monuments or displays of the Ten Commandments on public property is a practice that is "deeply embedded in the history and tradition of this country."[438] Moreover, unlike crosses, these monuments and images are acceptable to the vast majority of Americans, regardless of their personal faiths or lack thereof. There is no good reason to believe that these memorials are unconstitutional.

Religious Inscriptions on Public Buildings

Numerous public buildings contain biblical and religious inscriptions. In this section, I'll consider only structures in our nation's capital. Since its adoption in 1791, the First

Amendment has restricted the ability of the national government to pass laws respecting an establishment of religion, but there is little evidence that anyone raised constitutional or other objections to the inclusion of religious language on these public buildings when they were designed and built.

The most prominent structure in District of Columbia is the Washington Monument. It is capped with an 8.9-inch aluminum tip that faces east and is inscribed with the Latin words "'Laus Deo,' which translate to, 'Praise be to God.'"[439] Inside the monument, one can find "[o]ne hundred and ninety-three unique stone tablets [that] are set into interior walls of the Washington Monument, donated to the monument in honor of the Nation's first president."[440] Some of these include biblical verses such as Proverbs 10:7 ("the memory of the just is blessed"),[441] and phrases including "In God We Trust."[442] One includes a sculpted image of an open Bible.[443]

Biblical quotations and religious phrases can be found in numerous federal buildings. For instance, the Department of Agriculture's exterior northern wall includes a verse from II Timothy: "The husbandman that laboreth must be first partaker of the fruit" (II Tim. 2:6).[444] Similarly, the Library of Congress's Jefferson Building includes the following quotations: "What doth the Lord require of thee, but to do justly, to love mercy, and to walk humbly with thy God?" (Micah 6:8); "The Heavens declare the glory of God; and the firmament showeth his handiwork" (Proverbs 19:1); and "The light shineth in darkness and the darkness comprehendeth it not" (John 15:1).[445] As well, both chambers of Congress and the U.S. Capitol Visitors Center feature prominently the phrase "In God We Trust," and the Capitol's prayer room includes the inscription "Preserve me, O God: for in Thee do I put my trust."[446]

"In God We Trust" and "One Nation, Under God" and "So Help Me God"

In 1865, Congress authorized the inscription of "In God We Trust" on U.S. coins. In 1956, Congress made "In God We Trust" the national motto and directed that it be inscribed on all currency.[447] In 1954, Congress added the words "under God" to the Pledge of Allegiance so that it reads, "I pledge allegiance to the Flag of the United States of America, and to the Republic for which it stands, one Nation under God, indivisible, with liberty and justice for all."[448] Finally, the naturalization oath ends with the phrase "so help me God." No one may be compelled to say the Pledge of Allegiance or end their oaths with "so help me God" if they object to doing so, but that still hasn't stopped separationists from challenging all of these practices. To date, judges have not found their arguments to be persuasive.[449]

Memorials With Symbols/Language From Minority Faiths

At the beginning of this chapter, I mentioned that Ohio approved a Holocaust and Liberators Memorial, a central feature of which is a fractured Star of David.[450] The Freedom From Religion Foundation objected that including the Star of David violated the Establishment

Clause. The objection is particularly ridiculous given that the Holocaust was about erasing the Jewish people. Fortunately, the Ohio legislature ignored this complaint, and the memorial was dedicated on June 2, 2014.[451]

Other monuments with Jewish symbols exist throughout the nation. South Carolina's 2001 Holocaust Memorial features the Star of David prominently, as does New Orleans's 2003 memorial.[452] Philadelphia's monument to "Six Million Jewish Martyrs," on the other hand, depicts, according to Justice Alito, "a burning bush, Torah scrolls, and a blazing menorah."[453] Charleston, South Carolina's 1999 memorial contains as its "the central element" a "lonely discarded tallit, the Jewish prayer shawl used by men in the synagogue and also in which for some it was customary to be wrapped for burial."[454]

The United States Holocaust Memorial Museum in Washington, D.C. was built on land donated by the federal government and receives annual appropriations from Congress. Its Hall of Remembrance can be interpreted as referencing the Star of David, and passages from the Hebrew Scriptures are inscribed on the building's walls, including: "What have you done? Hark, thy brother's blood cries out to me from the ground!" (Genesis 4:10); "Only guard yourself and guard your soul carefully, lest you forget the things your eyes saw, and lest these things depart your heart all the days of your life, and you shall make them known to your children, and to your children's children." (Deuteronomy 4:9); "I call heaven and earth to witness this day: I have put before you life and death, blessing and curse. Choose life—that you and your offspring shall live." (Deuteronomy 30:19); and "You are my witnesses." (Isaiah 43:10).[455]

Idaho's Anne Frank Human Rights Memorial, dedicated in 2002, contains numerous religious inscriptions, including: "Let my people go" (Moses); "Let justice roll down like waters, and righteousness like an ever-flowing stream" (Amos); "What you do not want done to yourself, do not do to others" (Confucius);[456] "Not in the sky, nor in mid-ocean, in a mountain cave, is found that place on earth where abiding one may escape from the consequences of one's evil deed" (Buddha).[457]

As America becomes more diverse, the range of religious images and language used in public memorials is bound to expand. For instance, in 2001, New York City dedicated a tree and plaque to commemorate "the founding of the Hare Krishna religion in the United States." The plaque included "the group's distinctive sixteen-word mantra: 'Hare Krishna, Hare Krishna, Krishna, Hare Hare Hare Rama, Hare Rama, Rama, Hare Hare.'"[458] And, to give one last example, Justice Alito noted in his opinion in the Bladensburg Cross case that "a new memorial to Native American veterans in Washington, D.C., will portray a steel circle to represent 'the hole in the sky where the creator lives.'"[459] Such diversity is properly celebrated.[460]

America has a long tradition of erecting monuments that include religious symbolism and language. As the nation has become diverse, so have the symbols citizens have utilized to commemorate and memorialize people and events. Symbols may have different meanings, but crosses are often associated with Christianity, the Star of David with Judaism, and the Ten Commandments with Judaism, Christianity, and Islam. The United States Supreme Court has upheld the practice of erecting crosses and monuments of the Ten Commandments on public property. Justice Breyer and others have suggested that these monuments are constitutional, at least in part, because they were erected many decades ago.[461] However, to conclude that recently erected monuments with religious symbols violate the Establishment Clause would disproportionately impact symbols of minority religions, as almost every monument discussed in this section was created after 1990.

A rule that old monuments with religious language/symbols are constitutional, but new ones are not, would have the perverse effect of requiring the removal of the Star of David from Holocaust memorials on public property, while permitting the Bladensburg Cross to remain in place. It is reasonable to view even recently-erected monuments containing religious language and symbols as being "deeply embedded in the history and tradition of this country."[462]

The Constitution Does NOT Require a Secular Public Square

Communities must be free to engage in religious speech, recognize the existence of God, and celebrate religious holidays. An originalist understanding of the Establishment Clause protects these practices, as does the fact that they are deeply rooted in our country's history. Groups such as the Freedom From Religion Foundation will continue to attempt to deny communities these freedoms, even as they attack the ability of individuals to live according to their religious convictions. It is to these attacks that we now turn.

CHAPTER SEVEN

Why Tolerate Religion? The Future of Religious Liberty

America's founders embraced a robust understanding of religious liberty, and they protected it as a matter of constitutional law. Their primary strategy for protecting individual freedom from interference from the federal government was to strictly limit its powers, but as a redundancy, they added the Free Exercise Clause to the First Amendment, which reads, "Congress shall make no law...prohibiting the free exercise thereof." Because the national government largely remained within its enumerated powers until the New Deal, it seldom passed legislation that had the potential to restrict religious freedom. However, states sometimes passed laws that restricted religious liberty—especially the freedom of unpopular religious minorities.

This chapter explores how American jurists and legislatures have approached religious liberty claims from the mid-nineteenth century to the present day. Courts were initially not as protective of religious minorities as they should have been, but by the mid-twentieth century, they offered robust protection for what many founders called "the sacred right of conscience." In 1940, the United States Supreme Court applied the First Amendment's Free Exercise Clause to the states, and justices soon developed tests that provided good, but not perfect, protection to religious liberty. By the late twentieth century, conservatives and progressives alike agreed that religious liberty for all citizens must be carefully guarded. Additionally, numerous Christian legal advocacy groups such as the Christian Legal Society, Alliance Defending Freedom, Becket, and First Liberty were formed to protect the religious freedom of all citizens—Christians and non-Christians alike. Alas, since the turn of this century, political progressives have turned away from their earlier commitment to religious liberty, at least with respect to religious traditionalists. This is a mistake; the religious freedom of all citizens must be robustly protected.

The Mormon Cases and the Belief-Action Doctrine

Prior to 1940, the Supreme Court had decided only a few religious liberty cases, but it had heard several, including a few that arose in the federal territory of Utah. Then and now, the territory, and later state, was heavily populated by members of the Church of Jesus Christ of the Latter Day Saints (LDS)—colloquially referred to as Mormons.[463] Claiming to act upon a revelation of God, LDS president Joseph Smith secretly married multiple women in the 1830s, and soon, other LDS leaders did so as well. Announced as an official church doctrine in 1852, by 1860, 43.6 percent of families in the Utah territory were polygamous.[464] When word of this practice—

and abuses associated with it—reached Washington, Congress passed the Morrill Anti-Bigamy Act of 1862, which banned polygamy in the federal territories. Utah resident and LDS church member George Reynolds was prosecuted and convicted for engaging in the practice.

Reynolds appealed his conviction to the United States Supreme Court, arguing that the First Amendment protected his right to engage in polygamy because it was required by his faith. The justices unanimously rejected his appeal, explaining in an opinion by Chief Justice Morrison Waite that the Free Exercise Clause protected Reynold's ability to *believe* whatever he wanted, but that the national government could punish his *actions* (a rule that is referred to as the Belief-Action Doctrine). Waite observed that religious liberty clearly can't protect harmful practices such as human sacrifice or polygamy.[465]

Chief Justice Waite was correct that the First Amendment cannot protect practices like human sacrifice, but his belief-action dichotomy is inadequate. After all, the text of the Free Exercise Clause clearly protects the free *exercise* of religion. As we shall see, Justice William Brennan developed a far better test in 1963, but this came far too late to help Mr. Reynolds. In fact, the national government continued to put pressure on the LDS Church, pressure so intense it may fairly be called persecution. In 1890, church president William Woodruff had a "divine revelation" that led him to renounce polygamy and advise church members to "refrain from contracting any marriage forbidden by the law of the land."[466]

Sister Wives

Some Mormons refused to acknowledge LDS president Woodruff's "revelation" as valid. They founded offshoot denominations, including Apostolic United Brethren and the Fundamentalist Church of Jesus Christ of the Latter-Day Saints, and continued to practice polygamy. Utah's 1896 constitution prohibits polygamy in a provision that cannot be revoked "without the consent of the United States and the people of this State." Over the years, members of these offshoot sects have been successfully prosecuted in Utah and other states for practicing polygamy, although states often neglect to enforce these laws. In 2010, the television show "Sister Wives" began documenting the "marriage" of Kody Brown and his four wives (he claimed to be legally married to one of his wives and spiritually married to all four). The Browns belong to the Apostolic United Brethren, which considers polygamy to be a "core religious practice."[467] Utah authorities investigated their "marriage" but declined to prosecute. The Browns challenged the constitutionality of Utah's statute prohibiting polygamy, but the Tenth Circuit Court of Appeals refused to hear their case because the judges determined there was no real controversy. The Browns moved from Utah to Nevada and currently reside in Arizona. As of this writing (2022), the show is still being aired.

The Supreme Court Begins Protecting Religious Liberty

Most cases involving religious liberty occur at the state level and are resolved by state courts. States could be protective of religious minorities, but—as we saw in the last chapter—they were also quite harsh towards those perceived to oppose basic American values.[468] In the 1940 case of *Cantwell v. Connecticut*, the Supreme Court applied the Free Exercise Clause to the states for the first time.[469] If justices adhered to the belief-action distinction articulated in *Reynolds v. United States*, this might not have mattered, since virtually every threat to religious liberty involves a law targeting action, not belief. Fortunately, they did not.

Over the past one hundred fifty years, states have rarely passed statutes explicitly prohibiting religious acts. At the same time, it is not uncommon for states to pass neutral laws of general applicability that prevent people from acting on their religious convictions or force them to violate them. As America headed into the Second World War, in order to promote national unity, a number of states enacted laws requiring school children to salute and pledge allegiance to the American flag.[470] Most Americans have no objection to these practices, but Jehovah's Witnesses believe that they violate the Bible's command not to worship graven images (Exodus 20:4–5). In 1940, eight Justices ruled that the states' interest in promoting national unity permitted them to override these objections.[471]

Three years later, the Supreme Court returned to this issue. In a stunning reversal, six Justices concluded that states could *not* compel Jehovah's Witnesses to engage in these acts. In oft-quoted words, Justice Robert H. Jackson averred:

> The very purpose of a Bill of Rights was
> to withdraw certain subjects from the
> vicissitudes of political controversy, to
> place them beyond the reach of major-
> ities and officials and to establish them
> as legal principles to be applied by the
> courts. One's right to life, liberty, and
> property, to free speech, a free press,
> freedom of worship and assembly, and
> other fundamental rights may not be
> submitted to vote; they depend on the
> outcome of no elections.[472]

After considering the state's interest in forcing
students to salute the flag, Jackson concluded that:

> If there is any fixed star in our constitu-
> tional constellation, it is that no official,
> high or petty, can prescribe what shall
> be orthodox in politics, nationalism,
> religion, or other matters of opinion,
> or force citizens to confess by word or
> act their faith therein. If there are any
> circumstances which permit an excep-
> tion, they do not now occur to us.[473]

Justice Jackson's opinion relies on multiple provisions from the Bill of Rights and can be read to protect
both religious and non-religious citizens, but his argument is particularly compelling with respect to state laws
that require people to violate their religious convictions.
That most Americans do not view saluting the flag, and
pledging allegiance to it, as equivalent to worshiping a

graven image was properly determined by the Court to be completely irrelevant. Religious liberty protects the ability of citizens to act according to the dictates of their own consciences, not the consciences of others.

The Sherbert Test

In the 1963 case of *Sherbert v. Verner*, the Supreme Court developed a framework for thinking through how to accommodate religious objectors to general laws. Under the leadership of liberal Justice William J. Brennan, the Court adopted the principle that government actions that burden a religious practice must be justified by a compelling state interest.[474] Later, the Court added the requirement that this interest must be pursued in the least restrictive manner possible. In other words, citizens should not be forced to violate their religious beliefs unless it is absolutely necessary. Whenever possible, an accommodation should be found.

Religious citizens did not always win their cases under this test, which was regularly referred to as the Sherbert Test, but it certainly provided better protection than the belief-action test. The high watermark of the Supreme Court's Free Exercise Clause jurisprudence is often considered to be the case of *Wisconsin v. Yoder* (1972). The controversy involved Amish families who lived in New Glarus, Wisconsin. These citizens did not object to sending their children to public schools through the eighth grade, but they refused to send them to the public high school. Although Amish generally do not go to court to resolve disputes, an attorney acting on their behalf objected that the Free Exercise Clause required the state to exempt them from the state's compulsory attendance law. In 1972, a unanimous Supreme Court (with a partial dissent by Justice William O. Douglas) agreed. The justices conceded that states have an interest in requiring education but said that it is not compelling enough to override the religious convictions of these families.[475]

Who Are the Amish?

Huldrych Zwingli (1484–1531) was a leader of the Protestant Reformation in Switzerland. Among his followers were the Mennonites, from whom the disciples of Jakob Amman split in the early eighteenth century. Known as the Amish, these Christians are pacifists who reject modern technology such as phones, automobiles, and buttons (believing the latter to be ostentatious). Viewed with suspicion in Europe, many Amish immigrated to Pennsylvania in the eighteenth century and from there moved to other states, including Wisconsin.

Amish horse and buggy

Since 1972, states have liberalized their compulsory attendance laws and their regulation of private schools and homeschooling so that it is far easier to remove children from public schools. Moreover, the Supreme Court has allowed states to increase aid to these schools, thus making them more affordable.[476] These laws were changed for a complex set of reasons, but among them was the desire of legislators to accommodate citizens who desire a faith-based education for their children.

Sherbert Repudiated and Resuscitated

In 1990, a majority of Supreme Court Justices repudiated the Sherbert Test in *Employment Division v. Smith*.[477] The case involved a Native American who had a religious conviction that required him to use peyote in religious ceremonies. Although peyote is a controlled substance, the national government recognized its legitimate use in "bona fide religious ceremonies of the Native American Church" in 1966.[478] Many other states did as well, but my home state, Oregon, did not.

In *Employment Division v. Smith*, the Supreme Court ruled that the First Amendment does not shield Native Americans who use peyote in religious ceremonies from laws prohibiting its use. In his majority opinion, Antonin Scalia made it clear that states *could* create exemptions to protect religious minorities but that the Free Exercise Clause did not require them to do so. Shortly after this decision, Oregon passed a law to permit individuals to use peyote in religious ceremonies. In 1994, without any recorded objections, Congress amended the American Indian Religious Freedom Act to protect Native Americans in twenty-two states that did not permit Native Americans to use peyote in religious ceremonies.

The Supreme Court's decision in *Employment Division v. Smith* was widely criticized. Republicans and Democrats agreed that it was a dark day for religious liberty. Shortly after the decision was handed down, members of Congress drafted, proposed, and voted on a bill to restore the Sherbert Test. It is a testament to the consensus that the nation had reached that the Religious Freedom Restoration Act (RFRA) of 1993 passed in the House without a dissenting vote, was approved ninety-seven to three by the Senate, and was signed into law by President Bill Clinton. A few years later, Congress passed the Religious Land Use and Institutionalized Persons Act (2000), a major purpose of which was to protect the ability of prison inmates to freely exercise their religious convictions.[479]

Of course, not all religious practices should be accommodated. State and national governments sometime refuse to protect religious citizens or have even withdrawn protections when they determine that the actions in question are extremely damaging to the common good. For instance, beginning in the early twentieth century, many states accommodated parents who have religious objections to providing medical treatment for their children. However, when it became evident that children were dying from illnesses that medical advances had rendered easily treatable, some states repealed these protections.[480] Every state should do so.

Mary Baker Eddy and "Christian Science"

Mary Baker Eddy (1821–1919), published *Science and Health* in 1875. In it, she argued that physical ailments are illusions that should be treated by prayer alone. In 1879, she and a few adherents founded Church of Christ, Scientist. The denomination grew rapidly in the late nineteenth century but has shrunk dramatically since the Second World War (perhaps due to advances in the field of medicine). It is impossible to know how many children have died because their parents refused medical treatment for religious reasons, but one study found that the vast majority of the 172 children who were denied medical care between 1975 and 1995 died but would have survived if they had received proper care.[481]

Similarly, most states currently provide religious exemptions to vaccination requirements, but a number of them are currently debating whether they should be limited or repealed. This debate is entirely appropriate. Religious liberty is a very important American value, but it is not a trump card that wins every time. If states, or the national government, have compelling reasons to limit the ability of individuals to act upon their religious convictions, they may do so, but as we have seen, by the late twentieth century, a consensus had emerged that religious liberty was a core American value that should be robustly protected.

The Fall of Religious Liberty?

In the twenty-first century, this one-time consensus seems to be unraveling. Robert P. George of Princeton University, a leading student of the subject, observed in 2012 that there is "a massive assault on religious liberty going on in this country right now."[482] More recently, attorney David French wrote about "a trend where legal activists at all levels of government had been aggressively expanding their regulatory and ideological attacks on religious liberty."[483] Although most civic leaders and jurists remain committed to religious liberty in the abstract, support for protecting citizens from neutral laws that infringe upon religious convictions has deteriorated.[484]

For instance, the Obama Administration showed little concern for religious liberty when it required businesses to provide contraceptives and abortifacients to employees, even when the business owners had religious convictions against doing so. It also offered a rare challenge to the doctrine of ministerial exception, a legal protection which holds that religious groups should be free to choose, in the words of Chief Justice John Roberts, "who will preach their beliefs, teach their faith, and carry out their mission."[485] In both instances, the Supreme Court rebuffed the Obama Administration and protected religious citizens.[486]

In 2016, the U.S. Commission on Civil Rights issued a report that said religious accommodations should be virtually non-existent. The Commission's Chair, Martin R. Castro, remarked in his personal statement that

> The phrases 'religious liberty' and 'religious freedom' will stand for nothing

> except hypocrisy so long as they remain code words for discrimination, intolerance, racism, sexism, homophobia, Islamophobia, Christian supremacy or any form of intolerance.[487]

Reasonable people can disagree about the propriety of certain accommodations, but surely religious convictions should be treated with greater respect.

At the state level, a few small-business owners who have religious objections to participating in same-sex marriage ceremonies have been prosecuted for declining to do so. Courts in these states have given little weight to arguments that the religious liberty provisions of state or national constitutions offer these photographers, florists, and bakers any protection.[488] In 2015, when Indiana and Arkansas considered bills virtually identical to the national RFRA, at least in part to help protect such citizens, a virtual firestorm erupted.

The Supreme Court's decision in *Masterpiece Cakeshop v. Colorado Civil Rights Commission* (2018) made it clear that state agencies may not target believers and disparage their convictions.[489] The case involved Jack Phillips, a baker who declined to bake a cake to celebrate a same-sex wedding in 2012. Same-sex marriages were not legally recognized in the state at the time, but the couple planned to get married in Massachusetts and celebrate their union in Colorado. They filed a complaint with the Colorado Civil Rights Commission, which found probable cause of a violation and referred the case to an administrative law judge. This judge ruled against Phillips, and the Commission (which had referred the case to the judge—welcome to the bizarre world of administrative law!) upheld the ruling, as did the Colorado Court of Appeals.

In this case, *seven* justices agreed that the Colorado Civil Rights Commission acted with such obvious animus against Phillip's religious convictions that it violated the First Amendment's Free Exercise Clause. In the majority opinion, Justice Kennedy noted that one Commissioner described Phillips' "faith as 'one of the most despicable pieces of rhetoric that people can use'" and explained that it was constitutionally problematic to "disparage his religion in at least two distinct ways: by describing it as despicable, and also by characterizing it as merely rhetorical—something insubstantial and even insincere."[490] Kennedy also remarked that at the time of Phillips' hearing, other Commissioners had made similar comments and that no one on the CCRC seemed to understand that bias against religious faith was inappropriate.[491] This decision sends an important message that judges and other government officials cannot be overtly hostile to people of faith, but the decision may simply encourage anti-religious bigots to keep their animus to themselves.

The CCRC was far from alone in conflating religious conviction with hatred. In 2015, Michigan passed a sensible bill to protect religious adoption agencies that refused to endorse unmarried or LGBTQ couples for adoption. Instead, these agencies would refer these couples to other agencies that had no such objections. Without this protection, some religious adoption agencies in the state would have had to close their doors, thus decreasing the number of institutions dedicated to helping find safe homes for infants and young children. Alas, in 2018, the state elected Dana Nessel to be its Attorney General. Conflating the legislature's desire to protect religious liberty with "hate mongering" and "discriminatory animus," she refused to defend the law.[492]

In 2019, presidential candidate Beto O'Rourke proclaimed that he would strive to eliminate the tax-exempt status that churches and religious institutions enjoy (as do many non-religious but charitable institutions) if they oppose same sex marriage. He averred, "There can be no reward, no benefit, no tax break for anyone or any institution, any organization in America that denies the full human rights and the full civil rights of every single one of us."[493] It is surely problematic that a church, synagogue, or mosque could lose a generally available benefit, for upholding longstanding religious convictions about marriage.

The COVID-19 virus revealed an appalling lack of concern for religious liberty among some of the nation's civic leaders. Most notoriously, the governor of Nevada ordered that "a church, synagogue, or mosque, regardless of its size, may not admit more than fifty persons, but casinos and certain other favored facilities may admit 50 percent of their maximum occupancy—and in the case of gigantic Las Vegas casinos, this means that thousands of patrons are allowed."[494]

Civic officials in most states adopted COVID-19-related restrictions on religious services and other public meetings. A reasonable case can be made that states had compelling reasons to limit religious services during the pandemic, but what they cannot do is treat churches, mosques, and synagogues more harshly than businesses such as casinos. Governments must treat similarly situated enterprises equally. Some Christians argued that governments have *no* authority over churches, but such claims are ill-conceived. There is nothing theologically or constitutionally problematic when governments require churches to follow building codes, fire codes, criminal laws, and pandemic regulations that are neutral and generally applicable.

These examples (and many more could be given) make it clear that something has changed. Political progressives no longer believe that religious liberty deserves to be robustly protected, especially when it comes to religious citizens who have traditional views on human sexuality. Furthermore, it is not only progressive politicians who have abandoned religious liberty. In the academy, professors such Marci Hamilton, Brian Leiter, Richard Schragger, Micah Schwartzman, and John Corvino have made well-publicized arguments contending that citizens should seldom be exempted from generally applicable laws because of their religious convictions.[495] Between them, they offer four main arguments against religious liberty: (1) religion isn't special, (2) religiously motivated actions that harm others should not be protected, (3) majorities and corporations should not enjoy religious liberty, (4) religious exemptions violate the Establishment Clause. I'll consider each of these arguments, offer brief responses, and then suggest books and articles that offer far more extensive replies to these arguments.

Religion is not Special

In 2012, law professor Micah Schwartzman published an article in one of the nation's top law reviews entitled "What if Religion Is Not Special?"[496] The next year, University of Chicago law professor Brian Leiter published a book entitled *Why Tolerate Religion?*[497] Both works contend that there is no good reason to treat religion commitments as any more important than non-religious ones. A Muslim woman understands her faith to require her to wear a hijab; a fan believes his commitment to the Chicago Cubs requires him to wear a Cubs baseball cap. Why should the woman's conviction receive any more protection than that of the fan?

A simple response to these arguments is that religion is special insofar as it is specially protected by the First Amendment: "Congress shall make no law respecting an establishment of religion, of prohibiting the free exercise thereof..." and similar provisions in every state constitution. Legislatures have passed literally thousands of laws to protect religious, and only religious, citizens as well. To give just one example, Congress has long permitted religious pacifists who are drafted into the military to serve in alternative ways. This protection has never been extended by Congress to pacifists who are not religious.[498]

Schwartzman and Leiter recognize that religion is specially protected as a matter of law, but they make philosophical arguments that these protections are unjust. Christopher C. Lund offers an excellent response to such claims in an article entitled: "Religion Is Special Enough." Among other things, he observes that religion is extraordinarily important to many people—generally more significant than, say, a commitment to a sports team. In part because it is so important, a great deal of civil strife results when governments limit the ability of citizens to practice their faiths. Lund recognizes that religion may "not be uniquely special," but he argues persuasively that it is special enough to deserve robust protection.[499]

On a more positive note, religion does a great deal to promote the common good. Byron Johnson, Director of the Institute for Studies of Religion at Baylor University, observes that over

> the last several decades, thousands of studies published in peer-reviewed journals document that religion is associated with making people happier, healthier, better spouses, more generous, more ethical, more tolerant, and more active and responsible citizens.[500]

Many religious people are motivated by their faiths to found hospital, serve in food banks, work in homeless shelters, and so forth. Because religious liberty causes religion to flourish, those who care about the common good should advocate for religious freedom.[501]

Third Party and Dignitary Harms

Over the past decade, opponents of religious exemptions have argued that they should not be permitted if they harm third parties. For instance, Yale law professors Douglas NeJaime and Reve B. Siegel contrast the exemptions that permit Native Americans to use peyote in religious ceremonies that harm no third parties with exemptions that "protect women's access to contraception and abortion and from laws that protect LGBT people from discrimination."[502] So, for instance, when Barronelle Stutzman declined to create custom floral arraigments to celebrate a same-sex wedding ceremony, she harmed the couple seeking the flowers. As such, she should not be exempt from Washington's law banning discrimination of the basis of sexual orientation.

A good argument can be made that Stutzman was not, in fact, discriminating on the basis of sexual orientation, but let's focus on the claim that her refusal harmed the couple. The couple was not denied the ability to have flowers at their ceremony, even custom-made arrangements, as the vast majority of florists in Washington do not share Stutzman's conviction. Indeed, she referred the couple to three local florists who were willing to create arrangements to celebrate the wedding. The harm, opponents to exemptions in these cases say, is to the couple's "dignity."[503] The notion of a "dignitary harm" is recently coined and, as we shall see, is not particularly well thought out. We'll return to this concept, but first let's consider the claim that courts have held that religious liberty should not be protected if third-parties are harmed.

Concerns about third-party harms are nothing new. From the early colonies to the present day, religious pacifists have been granted exemptions from military service. Surely, increasing non-pacifists' chances of being drafted constitutes a harm to non-pacifists who do not wish to serve in the military. An unwilling draftee might well view this burden as substantially greater than the burden faced by a same-sex couple unable to obtain a custom floral arraignment from a particular florist.

Consider also the harms caused by speech protected by the First Amendment. The Supreme Court has ruled in favor of a constitutional right to burn the American flag as a form of political protest. It has also protected hateful demonstrations by members of the Westboro Baptist Church at military funerals. In both cases, the

Court has permitted these forms of free expression even though they are virtually certain to cause pain and give offense, especially to veterans.[504]

The perniciousness of third-party dignitary harms may be seen in current (2021–2022) debates over controversial statues in public places. Those who wish to tear down statutes of founding fathers, Confederate generals, and even Abraham Lincoln, often claim that the mere presence of these statues (or buildings named after these men) is offensive and an affront to their dignity. It is certainly appropriate to have orderly discussions about which historical figures communities choose to celebrate in public places, and perhaps some statues should be taken down. However, if the standard is that any statue that offends someone must come down, we will soon have a stark and naked public square.

Americans need to toughen up. If a baker has a religious objection to participating in a same-sex ceremony, the couple should go elsewhere.[505] If a coffee shop owner asks pro-life protestors to leave his establishment, they should go somewhere else.[506] The National Portrait Gallery has a bust of Margaret Sanger, the racist founder of Planned Parenthood. I am no fan of Sanger, but rather than advocate for its removal, the next time I visit the Gallery, I plan to glance the other way and walk by it.[507] That is not to say that we should not be profoundly concerned with respecting the dignity of others, but we cannot allow the subjective reaction of aggrieved parties to be used to deny some citizens the ability to act upon their religious convictions and/or engage in free speech.

Protecting Majorities and Corporate Religious Liberty

Another recently minted complaint is that the Supreme Court has begun to protect the religious liberty of majorities and corporations. Law professor Zoë Robinson, for instance, argues that since 1980, the Supreme Court's religious liberty jurisprudence "roughly mirrors contemporary public opinion, the views of the political branches, and the positions held by powerful social institutions (e.g., corporations)."[508] At first glance, it may seem odd to protect the freedom of corporations, so let's begin with this concern.

Law professor Steven D. Smith has observed that "corporate status is a legal construction that promotes the interest of the human beings who create and use" them.[509] Corporations have been recognized by the Supreme Court as "persons" for almost one hundred fifty years, and Congress specifically defines them as such.[510] Although a corporate entity itself may not speak, write, or worship, the men and women who created and are employed by it do. In other contexts, this is commonsensical. I have yet to meet a progressive who does not believe that entities such as The New York Times *Company* should be protected by the First Amendment. If it were not, the famous freedom of the press case *The New York Times Company v. Sullivan* (1964) would not have even been argued before the Supreme Court.[511]

Today, most churches and denominations are incorporated. Since the nineteenth century, courts have recognized that these entities are protected by the First Amendment.[512] This is problematic according to Professor Robinson, who is extremely troubled by decisions such as *Hosanna-Tabor Evangelical Lutheran Church and School v. Equal Employment Opportunity Commission* (2012).[513] This case involved the freedom of a corporation, Hosanna-Tabor, to decide, in the words of Chief Justice John Roberts, "who will preach their beliefs, teach their faith, and carry out their mission."[514] If the First Amendment does not protect the ability of religious entities to choose their own leaders and teachers without government interference, what does it protect? It should be completely irrelevant that Hosanna-Tabor is incorporated. Fortunately, a unanimous Supreme Court agreed that it is protected by the First Amendment.

Or consider the case of *Gonzales v. O Centro Espírita Beneficente União do Vegetal* (2005). The case involved a small Brazilian-based church whose members believe it is necessary to use hallucinogenic tea in religious ceremonies. When the federal government attempted to force the church to stop this practice, it sued under the Religious Freedom Restoration Act. Steven Smith asks a brilliant question about the case: "Was the religious group that sued under RFRA leading to the Court's unanimous decision...incorporated? Did anyone care? Should anything have turned on the question?"[515] It is not clear from the Court's opinion whether the church was incorporated or not, but it turns out that it is.[516] As in *Hosanna-Tabor*, justices unanimously agreed that *O Centro* was protected by the First Amendment.

But what about for-profit corporations? Concerns about corporate religious liberty skyrocketed after the Supreme Court held that Hobby Lobby—a family-owned corporation—could not be forced to provide insurance to its employees that covered drugs that may cause abortions. Justices ruled five to four that the Religious Freedom Restoration Act exempted Hobby Lobby from this mandate. The Green family, the owners of the corporation, were not attempting to stop women from purchasing these drugs; they simply had religious convictions that they should not be complicit in providing them. The Court recognized that the federal government could provide these drugs to women in other ways as well.[517]

Progressives complain that Hobby Lobby should not be protected by the First Amendment, but I have never heard one argue that this same logic applies to Crown Kosher Super Market, Inc., a small Jewish-owned business. The Market ran afoul of a Massachusetts law, "Observance of the Lord's Day," that required most businesses to be closed on Sunday. The owners of the store contended that the law placed an undue burden on them because their faith prohibited them from working on Saturday and the law prevented them from working on Sunday. Lawyers for the corporation claimed the law violated both the First and Fourteenth Amendments, but the Court ruled in *Gallagher v. Crown Kosher Super Market, Inc.* (1961) that the law was constitutional. The majority opinion was by liberal Chief Justice Earl Warren, three justices dissented, but no one argued that because Crown Kosher Super Market was a corporation that the Constitution did not apply to it.[518]

Sunday Closing Laws

In four cases decided in 1961, the Supreme Court upheld Sunday closing laws against a wide range of constitutional challenges.[519] These laws, known as "blue laws" because of the color of the paper upon which they were originally printed, have never been declared to be unconstitutional. Most states and localities have voluntarily repealed them, but some are still in effect. In Maine, for instance, car dealerships may not open on Sunday, hunting is not permitted on the Lord's day, and most large stores are prohibited from doing business on Christmas, Easter, and Thanksgiving.[520] Some private corporations, most famously Chick-fil-A and Hobby Lobby, voluntarily close on Sunday because of their owners' religious convictions. Relatedly, a number of states prohibit or limit the sale of alcohol on Sunday.[521]

Let's turn now to Professor Robinson's complaint, which is echoed by other scholars, that the Supreme Court has shifted from protecting minorities to majorities.[522] Those who make this argument sometimes assert that the First Amendment was intended to protect minorities.[523] This claim is misleading. The authors of the First Amendment believed that it applied to all Americans, not just minorities.[524] *In practice*, it has often been religious minorities such as Quakers, Mennonites, and Amish who have run afoul of neutral laws that nevertheless keep them from acting upon their religious convictions, and so have had to assert their First Amendment rights. This is not surprising, as majorities do a good job of protecting themselves through the democratic process. For instance, because self-identified Christians have controlled most state legislatures throughout the nation's history, it is not surprising that they adopted Sunday closing laws rather than Saturday closing laws. However, if a legislature had for some reason passed a Saturday closing law, surely Christians could rightfully challenge it on First Amendment grounds, just as Jewish citizens and corporations challenged Sunday closing laws.

Before proceeding, let's step back and consider what we mean by "majority" and "minority." Quakers, Mennonites, and Amish are all Christians, so one might categorize them as being as members of the majority religion in the United States. The florist mentioned above, Barronelle Stutzman, is a Southern Baptist. Only about 5.3 percent of Americans are Southern Baptists—hardly a majority.[525] One could, of course, lump Southern Baptists in with all Christians and then accurately say she is a member of a majority faith, but why do that for Southern Baptists and not Quakers?

The vast majority of Americans do not have religious convictions that would lead them to decline to participate in a same-sex wedding ceremony. Even in 2015 (when the Stutzman trial was to be held), 65 percent of Americans agreed that business owners should not be able to refuse to serve LGBT customers (even though doing so was illegal in only about half of the states).[526] The Alliance Defending Freedom surveyed a large number of florists in eastern Washington, where Stutzman lives, and found *no* other florist who shared her conviction.[527] As the case was being litigated, a spokesman for an LGBTQ advocacy group, Equal Rights Washington, observed that "there have been thousands of weddings...and this [the Stutzman case] is one of very few negative stories we've heard."[528] One might thus characterize Stutzman as a minority of one—i.e., the only Christian florist in eastern Washington who has religious objections to making a custom floral arrangement for a same-sex wedding ceremony.[529]

Rather than fretting about whether a complainant is part of the minority or majority, we would be far better simply insisting that the rights of all Americans must be protected whenever possible. Fortunately, the Supreme Court continues to share this opinion—and it continues to protect religious minorities. Robinson's claim that Court has shifted to "privilege" majority views is simply false. Consider, for instance, the following recent cases: *Gonzales v. O Centro* (2006) (protecting a small Brazilian-based church's use of hallucinogenic tea); *Holt v. Hobbs* (2015) (requiring a prison to permit an Islamic inmate to grow facial hair as required by his faith); *EEOC v. Abercrombie & Fitch* (2015) (holding a corporation accountable for refusing to hire a Muslim woman because she wore a headscarf, as mandated by her understanding of Islam); and *Tanzin v. Tanvir* (2020) (permitting three Muslim men to sue the FBI agents for damages under RFRA). These cases clearly cut against Robinson's argument, but rather than explaining why they do not, she simply ignores the first three (the fourth was handed down after she wrote her article). She also neglects the many recent lower court cases that have protected minorities.[530]

Simply put, religious corporations are legal persons protected by the First Amendment, and the rights of *all* Americans, whether they may be characterized as being in the minority or the majority, should be robustly protected.

Religious Liberty Advocacy Groups

The Christian Legal Society was founded in 1961. In 1975, it launched The Center for Law & Religious Freedom to defend and advance "all Americans' inalienable rights to religious freedom and life in the public square."[531] The Center was joined by other advocacy organizations, including the Alliance Defending Freedom (1993), Becket (1994) and First Liberty (1997).[532] The Christian Legal Society, the Alliance Defending Freedom, and First Liberty are explicitly Christian organizations, and many but not all of the attorneys at Becket are practicing Christians. All four organizations advocate for the ability of non-Christians to act upon their religious convictions. For instance, Becket represented Abdul Muhammad, the Islamic prisoner in *Holt v. Hobbs* 135 S. Ct. 133 (2015); and all of these groups routinely file *amicus* briefs on behalf of a wide range of individuals and organizations.[533]

Religious Exemptions Violate the Establishment Clause

Law professors Frederick Mark Gedicks and Rebecca G. Van Tassell, among others, have contended that religious accommodations (or at least some of them) violate the Establishment Clause.[534] Accommodations might be prohibited if the First Amendment erected a wall of separation between church and state, but it does no such thing. This constitutional provision was originally understood to prevent the evils associated with established churches.

Stanford law professor Michael McConnell agrees, and in an influential 2003 law-review article, he provides a succinct list of these evils:

A. government control over the doctrine and personnel of the established church;
B. mandatory attendance in the established church;
C. government financial support of the established church;
D. restrictions on worship in dissenting churches;
E. restrictions on political participation by dissenters;
F. use of the established church to carry out civil functions.[535]

Note that religious accommodations, even accommodations that favor specific denominations, are not on this list. Remarkably, the liberal justice William J. Brennan, in his concurring opinion in *Abington v. Schempp*, came up with a very similar list of practices the Establishment Clause was intended to prevent.[536] He then noted a number of practices supportive of religion that are constitutional, including "draft exemptions for ministers and divinity students."[537]

The Supreme Court has repeatedly ruled religious accommodations to be constitutional. To raise troops to fight in the First World War, Congress passed the Selective Service Act of 1917. The law exempted ministers of religion and divinity students from draft, and permitted members of historic peace churches such as the Quakers, Mennonites and Amish to do alternative, non-combat, service. Attorneys for Grahl Arver argued, among other claims, that these exemptions violated the Establishment

Clause. In *Arver v. United States* (1918), also referred to as *The Selective Draft Law Cases*,[538] Chief Justice Edward White dismissed this claim as absurd:

> And we pass without anything but state-
> ment the proposition that an establish-
> ment of a religion or an interference
> with the free exercise thereof repug-
> nant to the First Amendment resulted
> from the exemption clauses of the act to
> which we at the outset referred because
> we think its unsoundness is too apparent
> to require us to do more.[539]

White was absolutely correct: in no way, shape, or form does protecting the convictions of religious minori-ties constitute an establishment of religion. This is true even when accommodations are limited to members of specific denominations, as they were in the Selective Service Act of 1917, or when the national government protected the ability of Native Americans to use peyote in "bona fide religious ceremonies of the Native Amer-ican Church."[540]

It is constitutionally permissible for governments to protect only members of specific denominations, but as a matter of fairness, they should protect all reli-gious citizens. Fortunately, Congress remedied this error when it passed the Selective Training and Service Act of 1940, which exempted from combat duties anyone "who, by reason of religious training and belief, is conscien-tiously opposed to participation to war in any form."[541] It is noteworthy that representatives of the historic peace churches lobbied for the protection of *all* pacifists—whether members of their churches, other churches, or no church at all. As a matter of fairness, this protection should be extended to non-religious pacifists as well, but as noted earlier, so far Congress has not done so.

Arver v. United States should have made it crystal clear that religious accommodations are constitutionally permissible, but the Supreme Court has had to rule six times that religious exemptions do not violate the Establishment Clause.[542] In one unfortunate case, *Estate of Thornton v. Caldor* (1985), justices found an accommodation to violate the Establishment Clause. Ironically, the case involved a Connecticut statute that replaced its Sunday closing law with one stipulating that no "person who states that a particular day of the week is observed as his Sabbath may be required by his employer to work on such day."[543] This statute is far superior to a Sunday closing law because it ensures that Christians cannot be forced to work on Sunday, Jews cannot be forced to work on Saturday, Muslims cannot be forced to work on Friday, and so forth. Alas, the Supreme Court ruled eight to one that, because of the statute's "unyielding weighing in favor of Sabbath observers over all other interest," it violated the Establishment Clause.[544]

With the exception of this one case, the Supreme Court has always held that religious accommodations are constitutional, even in a case decided after *Estate of Thornton*.[545] This is entirely appropriate. An originalist understanding of the Establishment Clause does not prohibit accommodations. Indeed, the United States Constitution, which was approved only a year before the Bill of Rights was drafted, contains religious accommodations in Articles I, II, and VI, where it permits individuals either to swear or to affirm their oaths. The vast majority of citizens have no objections to swearing oaths, but Quakers and a few other religious minorities do. Recognizing this reality, America's founders placed religious accommodations in the nation's fundamental law.

In the First Federal Congress, James Madison proposed a version of what became the Second Amendment that stipulated that "no person religiously scrupulous, shall be compelled to bear arms."[546] This provision was approved by the House but rejected by the Senate. It does not appear in the Second Amendment, but Madison was able to add a similar proviso to the nation's first militia bill.[547] America's founders approved of and enacted a wide range of accommodations to protect religious minorities, and—as I demonstrate in an essay, "Religious Accommodations and the Common Good"— states and the nation have continued doing so.[548] This is as it should be, as accommodations permit governments to pass statutes to promote the common good *and* protect the ability of all citizens to act upon their religious convictions whenever possible.

Going Forward

In 1790, George Washington penned a letter to the "Hebrew Congregation" in Newport, Rhode Island. He wrote to this tiny religious minority that

> All possess alike liberty and conscience and immunities of citizenship. It is now no more that toleration is spoken of, as if it was by the indulgence of one

class of people, that another enjoyed the exercise of their inherent natural rights. For happily the Government of the United States, which gives to bigotry no sanction, to persecution no assistance requires only that they who live under its protection should demean themselves as good citizens, in giving it on all occasions their effectual support.[549]

This letter reflects well the founders' understanding that the religious convictions of *all* citizens must be respected. From the founding era to the end of the twentieth century, the nation and states became better at protecting this important right. Resisting those who would deny to some citizens the ability to act upon their religious convictions should be among our top political priorities. Additionally, readers might consider supporting one of the many fine organizations such as Alliance Defending Freedom, Becket, Christian Legal Society, and First Liberty that regularly fight for religious liberty in our nation's courtrooms.

James Madison's influence in the American founding is often overstated, but he must be recognized as an important advocate for religious liberty. Like Washington, he understood that all citizens possess this sacred and inalienable right. In 1820, Jacob de la Motta (c. 1789–1845), a prominent Jewish physician, gave a speech at the dedication of Savannah, Georgia's first synagogue. He sent a copy of it to Madison, who responded,

Among the features peculiar to the political system of the U. States, is the perfect equality of rights which it secures to every religious sect. And it is particularly pleasing to observe in the good citizenship of such as have been most distrusted and oppressed elsewhere, a happy illustration of the safety & success of this experiment of a just & benignant policy. Equal laws protecting equal rights are found as they ought to be presumed, the best guarantee of loyalty & love of country; as well as best calculated to cherish that mutual respect & good will among Citizens of every religious denomination, which are necessary to social harmony and most favorable to the advancement of truth. The account you give of the Jews of your Congregation brings them fully within the scope of these observations.[550]

America's founders believed that religious liberty must be robustly protected. If we desire to honor their memory, we must insist that this important right be robustly protected today.

CONCLUSION

In this book, I have argued that Christians motivated by their faith have done a great deal to advance liberty and equality in the United States. At times, progress has been far too slow, and upon occasion, some Christians motivated by religious concerns have actively worked against the freedom and equality of others.

Rather than review the argument of this book here, let me instead point out that this volume could be much longer. I might have followed the chapter on the abolitionists with one tracing the ongoing fight for racial equality through the Reconstruction Era and the Civil Rights Movement to the present day. Christians were often at the forefront of these movements, most notably ministers such as the Rev. Dr. Martin Luther King, Jr., the Rev. Ralph Abernathy, and the Rev. Andrew Young.

In Matthew 25, Jesus tells the parable of the sheep and the goats. He identifies a number of deeds performed by the sheep and neglected by the goats, including visiting and ministering to prisoners. When the criminal justice system works properly, men and women are in prison to be punished for committing crimes, so it is perhaps easy to ignore their needs. Christians, from Quaker advocates of prison reform in the nineteenth century to Charles Colson's effective ministry Christian Fellowship today, have been at the forefront of ministering to these needy souls. Rehabilitation, not punishment, should be the top priority for America's prisons.

Perhaps the greatest injustice of the past fifty years in the United States is the legalization of abortion. Forced on the entire country through the Supreme Court decision in *Roe v. Wade* and perpetuated by *Planned Parenthood v. Casey*, more than 62.5 million unborn children have been killed since *Roe*.[551] Christians have been among the most vocal opponents of this horrific practice, and we must continue to fight for the rights of those who are truly the "least of these" [Mathew 25:40]. Roman Catholics have long been opposed to the practice, but evangelicals were slow to recognize this great evil. Evangelical leaders including C. Everett Koop and Francis Schaeffer deserve great credit for mobilizing literally millions of evangelicals to oppose it.

At times, the battle to overturn *Roe v. Wade* seemed unwinnable. Critics of *Roe* were finally vindicated when the United States Supreme Court overturned the decision by a vote of 6-3 in the summer of 2022.[552] But overturning *Roe* only returns the issue to the states, which can ban, restrict, or promote the practice as they see fit. Opponents of abortion still have a great deal of work to do, work that includes supporting laws restricting or banning most abortions and ensuring that women who need help bringing their pregnancies to term receive it.[553]

American Christians have advocated for freedom and equality not only in the United States, but also throughout the world. Notably, writers such as Thomas Farr, Paul Marshall, and Nina Shea, along with civic leaders such as former Representatives Frank Wolf (R-VA) and Tony Hall (D-OH), have been successful in shining light on the persecution of religious minorities across the globe. These and other activists successfully led the charge for the International Religious Freedom Act of 1998.[554] These efforts have led to some improvements, but because of the rise of authoritarian leaders in China, India, Russia, and other countries, the fight is far from over.

Scholars and popular writers will undoubtedly continue to characterize Christians, particularly conservative Christians, as opponents of progress. But sometimes what is viewed as progress is anything but. I'm thinking particularly of the increasing domination of women's sports by biological males identifying as female, the willingness of parents and doctors to give harmful medication to children suffering gender dysphoria, and, in the worst cases, subjecting them to mutilating surgeries. Again, Christian leaders have led the battle against these practices—perhaps most famously Ryan Anderson, whose book *When Harry Became Sally: Responding to the Transgender Moment* was banned by Amazon.[555]

Let me close by acknowledging that, although important progress has been made, the United States has yet to live up to the majestic promises of the Declaration of Independence. The fight for liberty and equality was not won in the eighteenth, nineteenth, or twentieth centuries. It is ongoing, and all Americans—regardless of their religious convictions or lack thereof—should recommit themselves to it today.

ENDNOTES

1   Andrew Seidel, *The Founding Myth: Why Christian Nationalism is Un-American* (New York: Sterling, 2019), 17.

2   Seidel, Founding Myth, 124.

3   Matthew Stewart, *Nature's God: The Heretical Origins of the American Republic* (New York: W.W. Norton, 2014), 5-6.

4   Mark Lilla, *The Stillborn God: Religion, Politics, and the Modern West* (New York: Alfred A. Knopf, 2007), 58.

5   Rodney Stark, *The Victory of Reason: How Christianity Led to Freedom, Capitalism, and Western Success* (New York: Random House, 2005) and Tom Holland, *Dominion: How the Christian Revolution Remade the World* (New York: Basic Books, 2019). Holland explains in the preface to his book that he "was taken to church by my mother," that his "belief in God had faded over the course of my teenage years," but that his "morals and ethics" remain Christian (15-17).

6   Debra Utacia Krol. "After 400 years, Indigenous people reflect on the real story of the 'first Thanksgiving,'" azcentral., November 24, 2020, https://www.azcentral.com/story/news/local/arizona/2020/11/24/after-400-years-native-people-reflect-first-thanksgiving-real-story/6311708002/.

7 Daniel Webster, "The First Settlement of New England," in *The Great Orations and Speeches of Daniel Webster* (Boston: Little, Brown, and Company, 1906), 27.

8 Nathaniel Hawthorne, *The Scarlet Letter* (New York: Bantam Books, 1986), 44; Moses Coit Tyler, *A History of American Literature During the Colonial Time* (New York: P.P. Putnam's Sons, 1897), 1: 265.

9 H.L. Mencken, *A Mencken Chrestomathy* (New York: Alfred A Knopf, 1949), 624; Arthur Miller, *The Crucible* (New York: Penguin Books, 1952), 6.

10 Gregg Frazer, "The American Revolution: Not a Just War," *Journal of Military Ethics* 14 (2015), 45, 39; Seidel, The Founding Myth, 59-60; Mark Noll, Nathan Hatch, and George Marsden, *The Search for Christian America*, (Westchester: Crossway, 1983), 95-97.

11 Leviticus 25:10.

12 After much criticism of the first claim, *The New York Times* issued a partial retraction of this point even as it proclaimed that: "We stand behind the basic point." Jake Silverstein. "An Update to the 1619 Project," *The New York Times*, March 11, 2020, https://www.nytimes.com/2020/03/11/magazine/an-update-to-the-1619-project.html.

13 Brian Leiter, *Why Tolerate Religion?* (Princeton, NJ: Princeton University Press, 2013); Micah Schwartzman, "What if Religion Is Not Special?," *University of Chicago Law Review* 79 (2012), 1350-1427.

14 *Hosanna-Tabor Evangelical Lutheran Church & School v. Equal Employment Opportunity Commission*, 565 US 171, 196 (2012).

15 Daniel Webster, "The First Settlement of New England," in *The Great Orations and Speeches of Daniel Webster* (Boston: Little, Brown, and Company, 1906), 27.

16 Alexis de Tocqueville, *Democracy in America*, ed. Eduardo Nolla, trans. James T. Schleifer (Indianapolis: Liberty Fund Press, 2010), 1: 54, 49.

17 Debra Utacia Krol. "After 400 years, Indigenous people reflect on the real story of the 'first Thanksgiving,'" azcentral., November 24, 2020, https://www.azcentral.com/story/news/local/arizona/2020/11/24/after-400-years-native-people-reflect-first-thanksgiving-real-story/6311708002/.

18 Nathaniel Hawthorne, *The Scarlet Letter* (New York: Bantam Books, 1986), 44; Moses Coit Tyler, *A History of American Literature During the Colonial Time* (New York: P.P. Putnam's Sons, 1897), 1: 265.

19 H.L. Mencken, *A Mencken Chrestomathy* (New York: Alfred A Knopf, 1949), 624; Arthur Miller, *The Crucible* (New York: Penguin Books, 1952), 6.

20 Steven Waldman, *Sacred Liberty: America's Long, Bloody, and Ongoing Struggle for Religious Freedom* (New York: HarperOne, 2019), 10-12.

21 John Calvin, *Institutes of the Christian Religion*, 2 vols., trans. Ford Lewis Battles (Westminster: John Knox Press, 1960).

22 Initially, "everyone" primarily meant all males. But some Puritans recognized that "everyone" means everyone. So, for instance, the English Puritan Thomas Cartwright observed in the 1570s that "all ought to read the scriptures then all ages, all sexes, all degrees and callings, all high and low, rich and poor, wise and foolish have a necessary duty therein..." Quoted in David D. Hall, *Worlds of Wonder, Days of Judgement: Popular Religious Belief in Early New England* (Cambridge: Harvard University Press, 1990), 22.

23 R. A. Houston, *Literacy in Early Modern Europe: Culture and Education*, 2nd (London: Routledge, 2002), 158.

24 A great deal of information about literacy rates, both current and historical, is available here: https://our-worldindata.org/literacy. As Houston makes clear, literacy rates varied widely within regions of the same country, by social class, etc. Houston, *Literacy in Early Modern Europe*, especially 157-62.

25 Samuel Eliot Morison, *The Intellectual Life of Colonial New England* 2nd (Ithaca: Cornell University Press, 1956), 82–85. It is difficult to measure literacy rates in this era and calculations vary. Like Morrison, David D. Hall estimates that in the mid-seventeenth century the Puritans had achieved "near-universal literacy," Hall, *Worlds of Wonder*, 34, but Kenneth A. Lockridge calculates that 60 percent of males in New England were literate in 1660, and that this percentage rose to 85 percent by 1760. *Literacy in Colonial New England* (New York: W.W. Norton, 1974), 98, 13.

26 Morison, *The Intellectual Life*, 31.

27 Harvard College Charter (1650), available at: https://guides.library.harvard.edu/c.php?g=880222&p=6323072.

28 Henry Dunster to the Commissioners, 1645, quoted in Jeremiah Chaplin, *Life of Henry Dunster, First President of Harvard College* (Boston: James Osgood and Co., 1872), 80.

29 Morrison, *Intellectual Life*, 42.

30 Morrison, *Intellectual Life*, 33; Corydon Ireland, "Seal of approval," *The Harvard Gazette*, May 14, 2015, https://news.harvard.edu/gazette/story/2015/05/seal-of-approval/.

31 The exact definition of "separatist" is debated, but the one offered above is common. For further discussion see David D. Hall, *The Puritans: A Transatlantic History* (Princeton: Princeton University Press, 2019), 69-77.

32 Daniel L. Dreisbach and Mark David Hall, eds., *The Sacred Rights of Conscience: Selected Readings on Religious*

Liberty and Church-State Relations in the American Founding (Indianapolis: Liberty Fund Press, 2009), 86.

33 Dreisbach and Hall, *Sacred Rights of Conscience*, 86-87; Mark L. Sargent, "The Conservative Covenant: The Rise of the Mayflower Compact in American Myth," *New England Quarterly* 61 (June 1988), 233-51.

34 Suffrage was limited to males and, initially in Massachusetts Bay (but not Plymouth or Connecticut), church members, but a higher percentage of citizens could vote than at any other time or place that the world had seen to date.

35 Eric Nelson, *The Hebrew Republic: Jewish Sources and the Transformation of Political Thought* (Cambridge: Harvard University Press, 2010), 17.

36 Nelson, *The Hebrew Republic*, 28.

37 Nelson, *The Hebrew Republic*, 1–56. The failed Puritan colony of Providence Island was an exception to this rule. See Karen Ordahl Kupperman, *Providence Island, 1630–1641: The Other Puritan Colony* (New York: Cambridge University Press, 1993).

38 David A. Weir, *Early New England: A Covenanted Society* (Grand Rapids: Eerdmans, 2005). See also Daniel J. Elazar, *Covenant and Commonwealth: From Christian Separation through the Protestant Reformation* (New Brunswick: Transaction, 1996).

39 Quoted in Perry Miller, ed., *The American Puritans: Their Prose and Poetry* (New York: Columbia University Press, 1956), 89; Richard L. Bushman, *From Puritan to Yankee: Character and the Social Order in Connecticut, 1690–1765* (Cambridge: Harvard University Press, 1967), 154–159.

40 John Winthrop, "Speech to the General Court," (1645), in Miller, *The American Puritans*, 90–93. See also Joy B. Gilsdorf and Robert R. Gilsdorf, "Elites and Electorates:

Some Plain Truths for Historians of Colonial America," in *Saints and Revolutionaries: Essays on Early American History*, ed. David D. Hall, John M. Murrin, and Thad W. Tate (New York: W.W. Norton: 1984), 207–244

41 Miller, *The Crucible*, 6, 135.

42 That is, if a magistrate was excommunicated from his church, that excommunication did not affect his position as a magistrate. Dreisbach and Hall, *Sacred Rights*, 83–213.

43 Hall, *The Puritans*, 2.

44 *The Public Records of Connecticut* (Hartford: Case, Lockwood and Brainard, 1894), 2: 568.

45 Dreisbach and Hall, *Sacred Right*, 93.

46 Michael P. Winship, *Hot Protestants: A History of Puritanism in England and America* (New Haven: Yale University Press, 2018), 168.

47 Winship, *Hot Protestants*, 167.

48 Hall, *A Reforming People*, 151.

49 Hall, *The Puritans*, 236.

50 Edmund S. Morgan, *Puritan Political Ideas, 1558–1794* (Indianapolis: Bobbs-Merrill, 1965), xiii–xlvii, Dreisbach and Hall, *Sacred Rights of Conscience*, 89-102.

51 Hall, *Worlds of Wonder*, 6.

52 Hall, *Worlds of Wonder*, 6.

53 *Disestablishment and Religious Dissent: Church-State Relations in the New American States, 1776-1833*, ed. Carl H. Esbeck and Jonathan J. Den Hartog (Columbia: University of Missouri Press, 2019) provides an excellent account of religious establishments in early British, French, and Spanish colonies that eventually became American states.

54 Dreisbach and Hall, *Sacred Rights of Conscience*, 119.

55 *The Laws and Liberties of Massachusetts* (1648; reprint, San Marino: Huntington Library, 1998), 16.

56 Dreisbach and Hall, *Sacred Rights*, 98.

57 The colony of Rhode Island was the rare exception to this rule. Dreisbach and Hall, *Sacred Rights*, 118. In the Netherlands (Holland), some regions were fairly tolerant, but the country as a whole did not embrace a robust, modern conception of religious liberty. Evan Heafeli, *New Netherland and the Dutch Origins of American Religious Liberty* (Philadelphia: University of Pennsylvania Press, 2012).

58 Dreisbach and Hall, *Sacred Rights*, 98.

59 Dreisbach and Hall, *Sacred Rights*, 92.

60 Lord Acton to Mandell Creighton, April 5, 1887, published in *Historical Essays and Studies*, ed. J. N. Figgis and R. V. Laurence (London: Macmillan, 1907), 504.

61 Frohnen, *American Republic*, 15-22; Hall, *A Reforming People*, 107, 148; *The Laws and Liberties of Massachusetts* (1648; reprint, San Marino: Huntington Library, 1998), 46, 50. Virginia's *Articles, Lawes, and Orders* were printed in England in 1610-1611, but they are more akin to orders than legislation. See Dreisbach and Hall, *Sacred Rights of Conscience*, 84-86.

62 Winship, *Hot Protestants*, 167.

63 John Davenport, "A Sermon Preach'd at The Election of the Governour" (Boston, 1670), 4. See generally Alice M. Baldwin, *The New England Clergy and the American Revolution* (1928; reprint, New York: Frederick Ungar, 1965), 13–21. Similarly, two years earlier Jonathan Mitchel declared in his election sermon that "the Law of Nature, is part of the Eternal Law of God." Mitchel, "Nehemiah on the Wall in Troublesome Times..." (Cambridge, 1671), 11.

64 Samuel Nowell, "Abraham in Arms" (Boston, 1678), 10–11.

65 Nowell, "Abraham in Arms," 10.

66 John Witte provides a brief overview of this literature in his introduction to *Reformation of Rights*.

67 Shain, *Myth of American Individualism*, esp. 155–288.

68 Mencken, *A Mencken Chrestomethy*, 624.
69 John G. Turner, *They Knew They Were Pilgrims: Plymouth Colony and the Contest for American Liberty* (New Haven: Yale University Press, 2020), 122.
70 Turner, *The Knew They Were Pilgrims*, 132.
71 Turner, *They Knew They Were Pilgrims*, 131.
72 Winship, *Hot Protestants*, 160; S. Bryn Roberts, *Puritanism and the Pursuit of Happiness* (Woodbridge: The Boydall Press, 2015), 1.
73 Edmund S. Morgan, *The Puritan Family: Religion & Domestic Relations in Seventeenth-Century New England* Rev. ed. (New York: Harper Torchbooks, 1966), 16.
74 Morison, *The Intellectual Life of Colonial New England*, 35.
75 Robert Tracy McKenzie, *The First Thanksgiving: What the Real Story Tells Us About Loving God and Learning from History* (Downer's Grove: IVP Academic, 2013), 102.
76 Hawthorne, *The Scarlet Letter*, 206.
77 Hall, *Worlds of Wonder*, 210.
78 Hall, *Worlds of Wonder*, 210.
79 Hawthorne, *The Scarlet Letter*, 44; Tyler, *A History of American Literature*, 1: 265.
80 McKenzie, *The First Thanksgiving*, 131.
81 Francis J. Bremer, *The Puritan Experiment: New England Society from Bradford to Edwards* (Lebanon: University Press of New England, 1995), 186–199; Gilbert Chase, *America's Music: from the Pilgrims to the Present*, revised 3rd ed. (Urbana: University of Illinois Press, 1987), 3–37.
82 Samuel Willard, *A Compleat Body of Divinity* (Boston, 1726), 125.
83 John Cotton, *A Meet Help* (Boston, 1699), 14–15.
84 Edmund S. Morgan, "The Puritans and Sex," *New England Quarterly* (December 1942), 592–93.
85 Dreisbach and Hall, *Sacred Rights of Conscience*, 113.
86 Elton Trueblood, *The People Called Quakers* (Richmond: Friends United Press, 1966), 16.

87 Dreisbach and Hall, *Sacred Rights of Conscience,* 110–13; Trueblood, *People Called Quakers,* 14.

88 Carl E. Sigmond, "Quakers fight for religious freedom in Puritan Massachusetts, 1656-1661," last modified March 25, 2012, https://nvdatabase.swarthmore.edu/content/quakers-fight-religious-freedom-puritan-massachusetts-1656-1661.

89 "Religion and the Founding of the American Republic: America as a Religious Refuge: The Seventeenth Century, Part 2," Library of Congress, https://www.loc.gov/exhibits/religion/rel01-2.html.

90 Winship, *Hot Protestants,* 190.

91 Trueblood, *People Called Quakers,* 16, 1–84.

92 Winship, *Hot Protestants,* 258–59.

93 C.S. Lewis, *Mere Christianity* (New York: MacMillan Publishing Co., 1952), 26.

94 Emerson W. Baker, *A Storm of Witchcraft : The Salem Trials and the American Experience* (New York: Oxford University Press, 2016), 7; *Witchcraft in Europe, 400-1700: A Documentary History,* 2nd., ed. Alan Charles Kors and Edward Peters, revised by Edward Peters (Philadelphia: University of Pennsylvania Press, 2000), 17. Will and Ariel Durant, *The Age of Reason Begins* (New York: Simon and Schuster, 1961), 162–62; Brian P. Levack, *The Witch-Hunt in Early Modern Europe* (New York: Longmans, 1987), 20–28; Ann Llewellyn Barstow, *Witchcraze: A New History of the European Witch Hunts* (San Francisco: Pandora, 1994), 179–181.

95 Email correspondence with Daniel Nicholas Gullotta, July 23, 2020.

96 Will and Ariel Durant, *The Age of Voltaire* (New York: Simon and Schuster, 1965), 494.

97 Winship, *Hot Protestants,* 283; Baker, *A Storm of Witchcraft,* 202.

98   Winship, *Hot Protestants*, 284.

99   Winship, *Hot Protestants* 290. Emerson Baker elaborates on the many contingent factors that led to the trials which he aptly calls "a perfect storm." *A Storm of Witchcraft*, 6, xiv.

100   Hall, *A Reforming People*, 193.

101   Noll, Hatch, and Marsden, *The Search for Christian America*, (Westchester: Crossway, 1983), 95–97.

102   Noll, Hatch, and Marsden, *The Search for Christian America*, 97.

103   J. Daryl Charles and Mark David Hall, "The Just War Tradition and America's Wars," in Hall and Charles, *America's Wars: A Just War Perspective* (Notre Dame: University of Notre Dame Press, 2019), 4.

104   See also Noll, "Was the Revolutionary War Justified?" Christianity Today (February 8, 1999), 70; George Marsden, "The American Revolution," in Ronald A. Wells, ed., The Wars of *America: Christian Views* (Macon: Mercer University Press, 1991), 13–32; Noll, *In the Beginning Was the Word: The Bible in American Public Life, 1492-1783* (New York: Oxford University Press, 2016), 234–39, 271–329.

105   Gregg Frazer, "The American Revolution: Not a Just War," *Journal of Military Ethics* 14 (2015), 45, 39.

106   Gregg Frazer, *The Religious Beliefs of America's Founders: Reason, Revelation, and Revolution* (Lawrence: University Press of Kansas, 2012), 83; Frazer, "The American Revolution," 49–50.

107   Andrew Seidel, *The Founding Myth: Why Christian Nationalism Is Un-American* (New York: Sterling, 2019), 59–60

108   Frazer, "The American Revolution," 53; see also Frazer, *Religious Beliefs*, 66–106.

109   John Keown, "America's War for Independence: Just or Unjust?" *Journal of Catholic Social Thought* 6 (2009),

304, 298. See also John Fea, *Was America Founded as a Christian Nation?: A Historical Introduction* (Louisville: Westminster John Knox Press, 2011), 119–121; and John D. Roche, "'Fear Honor, and Interest': The Unjust Motivations and Outcomes of the American Revolutionary War," in Hall and Charles, ed. *America and the Just War Tradition*, 50–73.

110 See, for instance, John of Salisbury, *Policraticus* (New York: Cambridge University Press, 1990) (originally published in 1159).

111 This section draws from two articles I wrote with Sarah Morgan Smith: "Whose Rebellion? Reformed Resistance Theory in America, part 2," *Unio cum Christo* 4 (April 2018), 171–188 and "Whose Rebellion? Reformed Resistance Theory in America, part 1," *Unio cum Christo* 3 (October 2017), 169–184.

112 Gregg L. Frazer provides a good overview of loyalist arguments in *God against the Revolution: The Loyalist Clergy's Case against the American Revolution* (Lawrence: University Press of Kansas, 2018).

113 John Calvin, *Institutes of the Christian Religion*, ed. John T. McNeil (Philadelphia: Westminster Press, 1960), 2: 1519.

114 See, for instance, Willem Nijenhuis," The Limits of Civil Disobedience in Calvin's Last-Known Sermons: Development of His Ideas on the Right to Civil Resistance," in *Ecclesia Reformata: Studies on the Reformation*, vol. 2 (New York: Brill, 1994), 73–94.

115 See Smith and Hall, "Whose Rebellion? Reformed Resistance Theory in America, part 1," *Unio cum Christo* 3 (October 2017), 169–184.

116 Dworetz, *The Unvarnished Doctrine*, 160.

117 In *From Irenaeus to Grotius: A Sourcebook in Christian Political Thought: 100-1625*, ed. Oliver O'Donovan and

Joan Lockwood O'Donovan (Grand Rapids: Eerdmans, 2009), 701.

118   From *Irenaeus to Grotius*, 694.

119   John Goodman, How Superior Powers Ought to be Obeyed by their Subjects and Wherein They May Lawfully by God's Word be Disobeyed and Resisted (1558) as quoted in Writing The Early Modern English Nation. *The Transformation of National Identity in Sixteenth- and Seventeenth-Century England*, ed. Herbert Grabes, (Rodopi Bv Editions, 2001), 64.

120   Quoted in Quintin Skinner, *The Foundations of Modern Political Thought, vol. 2: The Age of Reformation* (Cambridge: Cambridge University Press, 1978), 2: 343.

121   Samuel Rutherford, *Lex, Rex, or The Law and the Prince* (1564; reprint; Harrisonburg: Sprinkle Publications, 1982), 33.

122   Michael P. Winship, *Hot Protestants: A History of Puritanism in England and America* (New Haven: Yale University Press, 2018), 178–192, 233–35; Francis J. Bremer, "In Defense of Regicide: John Cotton on the Execution of Charles I," William and Mary Quarterly 37 (1980): 103–124; John Cotton, *The Keyes to the Kingdom of Heaven* (London 1644; reprint Boston: Tappan and Dennet, 1843), 97–100.

123   Frazer, "The American Revolution," 48; Frazer, *God against the Revolution*, 2018, 12; Seidel, *Founding Myth*, 48, 59–60, 174.

124   Sydney E. Ahlstrom, *A Religious History of the American People* (Garden City: Doubleday, 1975), 1: 426

125   Harry S. Stout, "Preaching the Insurrection," Christian History 15 (1996), 17.

126   Charles Francis Adams, ed., *The Works of John Adams* (Boston: Charles C. Little and James Brown, 1850), 6: 4.

127   John Adams to F. C. Schaeffer, November 25, 1821, in Hutson, ed., *The Founders on Religion: A Book of Quotations* (Princeton: Princeton University Press, 2005), 15–16.

128 See, for instance, Alice Baldwin, *The New England Clergy and the American Revolution* (1928; Reprint, New York: Frederick Unger, 1958); and Mark David Hall, *Roger Sherman and the Creation of the American Republic* (New York: Oxford University Press, 2013), 53–62.

129 Douglass Adair and John A. Schutz, eds., Peter Oliver's *Origin and Progress of the American Rebellion* (Stanford: Stanford University Press, 1961), 41. "[D]issenting clergy," in this context, refers primarily to Reformed ministers, especially Congregationalists, Presbyterians, and many Baptists.

130 Paul Johnson, *A History of the American People* (New York: HarperCollins, 1997), 173.

131 John Leach, "A Journal Kept by John Leach, During His Confinement by the British, In Boston Gaol, in 1775," *The New England Historical and Genealogical Register* 19 (1865), 256.

132 The following section draws from the introduction to Hall and Charles, *America and the Just War Tradition*. The introduction provides an extensive and detailed treatment of the just war tradition, and the chapters following it consider each of America's major wars from a just war perspective.

133 Roche, "'Fear, Honor, and Interest," 63.

134 Roche, "'Fear, Honor, and Interest," 67.

135 Frazer, "The American Revolution," 37.

136 See, for example, Frazer, "The American Revolution," 37. And Frazer is correct that the taxes *were* light. On this point see Charles McIlwain, *The American Revolution: A Constitutional Interpretation* (New York: McMillan, 1923), 187.

137 These constitutional debates are brilliantly described by Barry Alan Shain, who also includes every relevant primary source document produced by American in-

tercolonial congresses between 1765 and 1777. See: *The Declaration of Independence in Historical Context: American State Papers, Petitions, Proclamations & Letters of the Delegates to the First National Congresses*, ed. Barry Alan Shain (New Haven: Yale University Press, 2014).

138   Bruce Frohnen, *The American Republic: Primary Sources* (Indianapolis: Liberty Fund Press, 2002), 92.

139   Robert Middlekauff, *The Glorious Cause: The American Revolution 1763-1789* (New York: Oxford University Press, 2005), 64.

140   Shain, *Declaration of Independence*, 88–94.

141   Shain, *Declaration of Independence*, 128–29.

142   "Speech Against the Stamp Act," Monticello Digital Classroom, https://classroom.monticello.org/media-item/speech-against-the-stamp-act/.

143   Middlelkauff, *That Glorious Cause*, 121.

144   Shain, *Declaration of Independence*, 466. See also the pamphlets published in *The Crises: A British Defense of American Rights: 1775-1776*, ed. Neil L. York (Indianapolis: Liberty Fund Press, 2016).

145   Edmund Burke, "An Appeal from the New to the Old Whigs," [1791] in *Further Reflections on the Revolution in France*, ed. Daniel E. Ritchie (Indianapolis: Liberty Fund Press, 1992), 107.

146   Most prominently, James Wilson, "Consideration on the Nature and Extent of the Legislative Authority of the British Parliament," in *Collected Works of James Wilson*, ed. Kermit L. Hall and Mark David Hall (Indianapolis: Liberty Fund Press, 2007), 1: 3–31 (penned in 1768 but not published until 1774); John Adams, "Novanglus" essays, in *The Political Writings of John Adams*, ed. George A. Peek (New York: Macmillan, 1954), 26–79; and Thomas Jefferson, "A Summary View of the Rights of British America," in *The Papers of Thomas*

Jefferson, ed. Julian P. Boyd, et al. (Princeton: Princeton University Press, 1950), 1: 121–137.

147 Shain, *Declaration of Independence,*135–36.

148 Shain, *Declaration of Independence*, 254.

149 Burke, "An Appeal from the New to the Old Whigs," 108.

150 Charles McIlwain, *The American Revolution*; Barbara Black, "The Constitution of Empire: The Case for the Colonists," *University of Pennsylvania Law Review* 124 (1976), 1157–1211; and John Phillip Reid, *Constitutional History of the American Revolution* 4 vol. (Madison: University of Wisconsin Press, 1986–1993).

151 Daniel L. Dreisbach and Mark David Hall, *The Sacred Rights of Conscience: Selected Readings on Religious Liberty and Church-State Relations in the American Founding* (Indianapolis: Liberty Fund Press, 2009), 311.

152 Frazer, "The American Revolution," 37.

153 Rodney Stark and Roger Finke, "American Religion in 1776: A Statistical Portrait," 49 (Spring 1988), 39–41.

154 Carl Bridenbaugh, *Mitre and Sceptre: Transatlantic Faiths, Ideas, Personalities, and Politics: 1689-1775* (New York: Oxford University Press, 1962).

155 Frohnen, *American Republic*, 110.

156 Roger Sherman to William Samuel Johnson, 1768, in Lewis Boutell, *The Life of Roger Sherman* (Chicago: A.C. McClurg, 1896), 65, 66.

157 Thomas S. Kidd, *God of Liberty: A Religious History of the American Revolution* (New York: Basic Books, 2010), 66.

158 John Adams to Jedidiah Morse, Dec. 2, 1815, quoted in Carl Bridenbaugh, *Mitre and Sceptre*, 233.

159 Alan Heimert, *Religion and the American Mind: From the Great Awakening to the Revolution* (Cambridge: Harvard University Press, 1966), 351–52; *Bernard Ba-*

ilyn, The Ideological Origins of the American Republic (Cambridge: Harvard University Press, 1967), 95–96.

160 Samuel Sherwood, "The Church's Flight into the Wilderness..." (1776), in Ellis Sandoz, ed., *Political Sermons of the American Founding Era: 1730-1805*, 2nd ed., (Indianapolis: Liberty Fund Press, 1998), 1: 514; *Thomas S. Kidd, The Protestant Interest*, (New Haven: Yale University Press, 2004); and Kidd, *God of Liberty*, 57–74.

161 Shain, *Declaration of Independence*, 214.

162 Shain, *Declaration of Independence*, 194. Official state papers produced by Congress, as well as private correspondence, petitions, and other texts routinely complained that the religious freedom of the colonists were under assault. For instance, see Shain, *Declaration*, 197–98, 207.

163 Shain, *Declaration of Independence*, 148, 207, 241

164 Shain, *Declaration of Independence*, 287–293, 358–59, 369–73, 383–86, 466–67. For an excellent discussion of these issues see Pauline Maier, *American Scripture: Making the Declaration of Independence* (New York: Alfred A. Knopf, 1997), 3–46.

165 Moses Mather, "An Appeal to the Impartial World (Hartford, 1775) in Ellis Sandoz, ed., *Political Sermons of the American Founding Era, 1735–1805*, 2nd ed. (Indianapolis: Liberty Fund Press, 1998), 1: 489.

166 Shain, *Declaration of Independence*, 490.

167 "The Gettysburg Address," UShistory.org, July 4, 1995, https://www.ushistory.org/documents/gettysburg.htm.

168 Shain, *Declaration of Independence*, 490–93.

169 Shain, *Declaration of Independence*, 490.

170 Frazer, "The American Revolution," 48–51.

171 Sarah Morgan Smith and Mark David Hall, "Whose Rebellion? Reformed Resistance Theory in America: Part II," *Unio cum Christo* 4 (April 2018): 171-188.

172 Maier, *American Scripture*, 3–46; Hall, *Roger Sherman*, 41–62. After the shooting began, British leaders made several different proposals to end the conflict, but on terms that the patriots found to be unacceptable. See Shain, *Declaration of Independence*, 318–338, 542–69, 657–669. In Barry Shain's estimation, "Britain refused to address the constitutional issues at the heart of the Imperial Crises, instead making conciliatory offers that were consistently too little and too late," 384.

173 Quoted in Don Cook, *The Long Fuse: How England Lost the American Colonies, 1760-1785* (New York: The Atlantic Monthly Press, 1995), xii.

174 Keown, "America's War for Independence," 302.

175 Shain, *Declaration of Independence*, 490.

176 Available at: https://www.nytimes.com/interactive/2019/12/20/magazine/1619-intro.html.

177 Mark Galli, "A Great and Terrible Nation," *Christianity Today*, July 3, 2018, https://www.christianitytoday.com/ct/2018/july-web-only/july-4-christian-nation-great-terrible-galli.html. See also Richard T. Hughes, *Myths America Lives By*, (Urbana: University of Illinois Press, 2003), 79; Mark A. Noll, Nathan O. Hatch, and George M. Marsden, *The Search for Christian America* (Westchester: Crossway, 1983); 97–100; John Fea, *Was America Founded as a Christian Nation?* (Louisville: Westminster John Knox, 2011), 153–54.

178 A good, accessible overview of how white Christians have participated in the evils of slavery and racism throughout American history is Jemar Tisby, *The Color of Compromise: The Truth About the American Church's Complicity in Racism* (Grand Rapids: Zondervan, 2019).

179 Corey Plante, "There Are 46 Million Slaves in the World – Here's Where They're Found," Inverse, May

12, 2017, https://www.inverse.com/article/31386-coun-tries-with-the-most-slaves?fbclid=IwAR2VFiuul-riC50f85t6KsIhOJRs3G-72zEniibRoaTvtmqha68Y-TXZxVArM.

180 Wendy Warren, *New England Bound: Slavery and Colonization in Early America* (New York: W.W. Norton, 2016), 110.

181 There is some dispute about the legal status of the Africans brought to America in 1619, but within a few years it is indisputably the case that Africans were held in slavery throughout British North America.

182 Nikole Hannah-Jones, "Our democracy's founding ideals were false when they were written," *The New York Times,* August 14, 2019, https://www.nytimes.com/interactive/2019/08/14/magazine/black-history-ameri-can-democracy.html.

183 "Slavery" was sometimes called by different names, and of course conditions varied. For instance, "serfs" in some regions could be bought and sold well into the nineteenth century.

184 Michael P. Winship, *Hot Protestants: A History of Puritanism in England and America* (New Haven: Yale University Press, 2018), 167–68.

185 Daniel L. Dreisbach and Mark David Hall, *The Sacred Rights of Conscience: Selected Readings on Religious Liberty and Church-State Relations in the American Founding* (Indianapolis: Liberty Fund Press, 2009), 92–93.

186 Warren, *New England Bound*, 10. New Englanders enslaved Native Americans as well, and some benefited from the slave trade. My point is simply that slavery was never as important in New England as it became in the American South.

187 This was true even in the American South. See, Eugene Genovese, *A Consuming Fire: The Fall of the Con-*

federacy in the Mind of the White Christian South (Athens: University of Georgia Press, 1998), 76–91.

188   "Go Down Moses" in Kai Wright, ed., *The African American Experience: Through Speeches, Letters, Editorials, Poems, Songs, and Stories* (New York: Black Dog & Leventhal Publishers, 2009), 306–307.

189   "Nobel Lecture," Nobelprize.org, https://www.nobelprize.org/prizes/peace/1964/king/lecture/.

190   And not all slaves were owned by white Americans—some free African Americans and Native Americans owned slaves as well. According to the 1790 census, there were 697,681 slaves and 3,929,214 white Americans. Available at: https://www2.census.gov/prod2/decennial/documents/1790m-02.pdf. Like any sensible person, I find the idea that one person can "own" another to be abhorrent, but it would be anachronistic to pretend that enslaved persons were not considered to be the property of their masters in this era.

191   Some but not all opponents of slavery also held racist views. The argument of this chapter is not that the founders were good, twenty-first century egalitarians, it is that many of them understood that slavery was unjust and desired to abolish the institution. Paul J. Polgar demonstrates that many abolitionists in this era opposed both slavery and racism in *Standard Bearers of Equality: America's First Abolition Movement* (Chapel Hill: University of North Carolina Press, 2019).

192   On Dickinson, see my essay "John Dickinson: Friend of Conscience," available at: http://www.libertylawsite.org/2018/07/17/john-dickinson-friend-of-conscience/.

193   Hall, *Political and Legal Philosophy of James Wilson*, 30.

194   Arthur Zilversmit, *The First Emancipation: The Abolition of Slavery in the North* (Chicago: University of Chicago Press, 1967), 167.

195 Gordon S. Wood, *The Americanization of Benjamin Franklin* (New York: Penguin Press, 2004), 226–29; Alan Houston, *Benjamin Franklin and the Politics of Improvement* (New Haven: Yale University Press, 2008), 200–16.

196 Rush, "An Address" (Boston: John Boyles, 1773), 30.

197 *George Washington: A Collection*, ed. W.B. Allen (Indianapolis: Liberty Classics, 1988), 319.

198 Quoted in Thomas West, *Vindicating the Founders: Race, Sex, Class, and Justice in the Origins of America* (Lanham: Rowman and Littlefield, 1997), 5. The first chapter in this book offers an excellent treatment of the founders and slavery.

199 Quoted in Thomas Kidd, *God of Liberty: A Religious History of the American Revolution* (New York: Basic Books, 2010), 147.

200 West, *Vindicating the Founders*, 10–14.

201 Peter Kolchin, *American Slavery: 1619-1877* (New York: Hill and Wang, 1993), 76.

202 The United States Code begins with what it labels as four "Organic Laws." These are the three documents listed above and the Articles of Confederation (1781). An organic law is a basic, foundational law as opposed to a regular statute.

203 Frohnen, *The American Republic*, 189.

204 Jake Silverstein, "Why We Published the 1619 Project," *The New York Times* (New York, NY), Dec. 20, 2019, https://www.nytimes.com/interactive/2019/12/20/magazine/1619-intro.html.

205 Tisby, *The Color of Compromise*, 42.

206 Jefferson freed a handful of slaves, including four who were likely children he had with Sally Hemings, an enslaved woman at Monticello. Jefferson may have desired to free more of his slaves, but debts from his

lavish lifestyle prevented him from doing so. On Jefferson and Hemings, see Annette Gordon-Reed, *The Hemingses of Monticello: An American Family* (New York: Norton, 2008) and *Thomas Jefferson and Sally Hemings: An American Controversy* (Charlottesville: University Press of Virginia, 1997).

207 "Declaring Independence: Drafting the Documents," Library of Congress, https://www.loc.gov/exhibits/declara/ruffdrft.html.

208 "Bill to Prevent the Importation of Slaves, &c.," Founders Online, https://founders.archives.gov/documents/Jefferson/01-02-02-0019. This bill did not pass in 1777, but Virginia banned the importation of slaves the next year.

209 Kevin Gutzman, "Reclaiming 1619," Law & Liberty, October 2, 2019, https://lawliberty.org/reclaiming-1619/; and Gutzman, *Thomas Jefferson – Revolutionary: A Radical's Struggle to Remake America* (New York: St. Martin's Press, 2017), 125–173.

210 *The Portable Thomas Jefferson*, ed. Merrill D. Peterson (New York: Penguin Books, 1975), 215.

211 *The Portable Thomas Jefferson*, 186.

212 A possibility that may have been validated, at least in Jefferson's mind, by the Haitian Revolution of 1791–1804. Gutzman, *Thomas Jefferson*, 155–56.

213 *The Portable Thomas Jefferson*, 186

214 Thomas Jefferson to John Holmes, April 22, 1820, in *The Portable Jefferson*, 568.

215 Gutzman, *Thomas Jefferson*, 169.

216 Jenny Bourne, "Slavery in the United States," EH.net, March 26, 2008, https://eh.net/encyclopedia/slavery-in-the-united-states/.

217 Quoted in Kidd, *God of Liberty*, 148.

218 Simon J. Gilhooley, *The Antebellum Origins of the Modern Constitution: Slavery and the Spirit of the American*

Founding (New York: Cambridge University Press, 2020), 42–86; Alexander Tsesis, *For Liberty and Equality: The Life and Times of the Declaration of Independence* (New York: Oxford University Press, 2012).

219 Frederick Douglass, "What to the Slave is the 4th of July?," in Ted Widmer, ed., *American Speeches: Political Oratory from Patrick Henry to Barack Obama* (New York: Library of America Paperback Classics, 2011), 76.

220 "Fragment on the Constitution and the Union," Collected Works of Abraham Lincoln, https://quod.lib.umich.edu/l/lincoln/lincoln4/1:264?rgn=div1;view=fulltext.

221 "Report on Government for Western Territory; March 1, 1784," The Avalon Project, https://avalon.law.yale.edu/18th_century/jeffrep1.asp.

222 "Northwest Ordinance; July 13, 1787," The Avalon Project, https://avalon.law.yale.edu/18th_century/nworder.asp.

223 Richard Beeman, *Plain, Honest Men: The Making of the American Constitution* (New York: Random House, 2009), 308–36; Max Farrand, *The Records of the Federal Convention of 1787* (New Haven: Yale University Press, 1937), 2: 219, 364, 370, 417, 372.

224 Quoted in Gary L. Gregg II and Mark David Hall, *America's Forgotten Founders*, 2nd (Wilmington: ISI Books, 2012), 56.

225 Farrand, *Records*, 2: 220, 221; 1: 201, 586–587; 2: 220–221, 374, 416–417

226 Farrand, *Records*, 2: 364.

227 Farrand, *Records*, 2: 364.

228 Farrand, *Records*, 2: 364.

229 Farrand, *Records*, 2: 370.

230 Zilversmit, *The First Emancipation*.

231 Farrand, *Records*, 2: 371.

232 Beeman, *Plain, Honest Men*, 215–218; Hutson, *Supplement*, 321; Farrand, *Records* 2: 148, 439.

233 Farrand, *Records*, 2: 364.

234 Farrand, *Records*, 2: 417.

235 Gutzman, *Thomas Jefferson*, 163.

236 Zilversmit, *The First Emancipation* and Joanne Pope Melish, *Disowning Slavery: Graduate Emancipation and "Race" in New England, 1780–1860* (Ithaca: Cornell University Press, 1998).

237 Polgar, *Standard Bearers of Equality*, 168.

238 *The First Laws of the Commonwealth of Pennsylvania*, ed. John D. Cushing (Wilmington: Michael Glazier, 1984), 282.

239 David Brian Robertson, "Madison's Opponents and Constitutional Design," *American Political Science Review*, 99 (May 2005): 225–243, 242.

240 I provide an extensive account of these revisions in *Roger Sherman and the Creation of the American Republic*, 77–91.

241 Mark David Hall, ed., *Collected Works of Roger Sherman* (Indianapolis: Liberty Fund Press, 2016), 321.

242 Dreisbach and Hall, *Sacred Rights*, 246.

243 Zilvermit, *The First Emancipation*, 114.

244 Zilvermit, *The First Emancipation*, 115.

245 Marcus Rediker, *The Amistad Rebellion: An Atlantic Odyssey of Slavery and Freedom* (New York: Penguin Books, 2013).

246 Quoted in Matthew Mason, "John Quincy Adams and the Tangled Politics of Slavery," in *Blackwell Companions to American History: A Companion to John Adams and John Quincy Adams* (West Sussex: Wiley Blackwell, 2013), 406.

247 Farrand, *Records*, 2: 371.

248 Daniel Webster, *Effects of Slavery on Moral and Industry* (Harford, 1793).

249 Webster, *Effects of Slavery*, 33, 5.

250 Webster, *Effects of Slavery*, 22.

251 See, for instance, Paul Finkelman, "The Founders and Slavery: Little Ventured, Little Gained," *Yale Journal of Law and Humanities*, 13 (2001), 417–19 and the scholarship cited there.

252 Joyce Appleby, *Inheriting the Revolution: The First Generation of Americans* (Cambridge: Harvard University Press, 2000), 235–250; Kolchin, *American Slavery*, 94–95.

253 Constance Green, *Eli Whitney and the Birth of American Technology* (Boston: Brown and Company, 1956), 40–62.

254 See, for instance, John C. Calhoun's speech on February 6, 1837 in *Union and Liberty: The Political Philosophy of John C. Calhoun*, ed. Ross M. Lence (Indianapolis: Liberty Fund, 1992, 461–476. See also Matthew Mason, *Slavery and Politics in the Early American Republic* (Chapel Hill: University of North Carolina Press, 2006), 21.

255 Jemar Tisby, *The Color of Compromise: The Truth About the American Church's Complicity in Racism* (Grand Rapids: Zondervan, 2019), 17.

256 Carolyn DuPont, *Mississippi Praying: Southern White Evangelicals and the Civil Rights Movement* (New York: New York University Press, 2013), 5.

257 Mark A. Noll, *A History of Christianity in the United States and Canada* (Grand Rapids: Eerdmans, 1992), 153.

258 Noll, *A History of Christianity*, 153; Richard Carwardine, *Evangelicals and Politics in Antebellum America* (New Haven: Yale University Press, 1993), 4–5.

259 Christine Leigh Heyrman, *Southern Cross: The Beginnings of the Bible Belt* (New York: Knopf, 1997). Although many Southerners were not evangelical,

southern women participated in reform movements (albeit at lower rates than northerners). See Elizabeth R. Varon, *We Mean to be Counted: White Women and Politics in Antebellum Virginia* (Chapel Hill: University of North Carolina Press, 1998).

260 Lyman Beecher in *The Autobiography of Lyman Beecher*, ed. Barbara Cross (1864, reprint. Cambridge: Harvard University Press, 1961), 411–18. Similar definitions have been used by Carwardine, *Evangelicals and Politics in Antebellum America*, 2–3 and Thomas Kidd, *Who Is an Evangelical? The History of a Movement in Crisis* (New Haven: Yale University Press, 2019), 4. Of course, evangelicals were not, and are not now, a monolithic. Especially noticeable in antebellum America are differences related to race and geographic region.

261 Curtis D. Johnson, *Redeeming America: Evangelicals and the Road to the Civil War* (Chicago: Ivan R. Dee, 1993), 4; David Masci and Gregory A. Smith, "5 facts about U.S. evangelical Protestants," *Pew Research Center*, March 1, 2018, https://www.pewresearch.org/fact-tank/2018/03/01/5-facts-about-u-s-evangelical-protestants/.

262 Timothy L. Smith, *Revivalism and Social Reform: In Mid-Nineteenth-Century America* (New York: Abingdon Press, 1957), 236. There are many variations of these eschatological views. I have attempted to sketch aim the major differences between two major approaches that are most relevant to politics.

263 Non-evangelical Christians participated in many of these organizations, but evangelicals usually dominated them. In this chapter, I highlight a number of individuals, all of whom identified as Christian—most of whom were orthodox Christians, and many, but not all of whom, were evangelicals.

264 This chapter only scratches the surface of these antebellum reform movements, even with respect to slavery and Indian removal. Good, accessible overviews of these movements include Ronald G. Walters, *American Reformers: 1815-1860*. Rev. ed. (New York: Hill and Wang, 1997); Carwardine, Evangelicals and Politics in Antebellum America; James Brewer Stewart, *Holy Warriors: The Abolitionists and American Slavery* (New York: Hill and Wang, 1997); Steve Inskeep, *Jacksonland: President Andrew Jackson, Cherokee Chief John Ross, and a Great American Land Grab* (New York: Penguin Press, 2015).

265 Essays profiling the political activities of Adams and Warren are available in Daniel L. Dreisbach, Mark David Hall, and Jeffry H. Morrison, ed., *The Forgotten Founders on Religion and Public Life* (Notre Dame: University of Notre Dame Press, 2009).

266 Sandra F. VanBurkleo, *"Belonging to the World": Women's Rights and American Constitutional Culture* (New York: Oxford University Press, 2001), 59–124; Julie Roy Jeffrey, *The Great Silent Army of Abolitionism: Ordinary Women in the Antislavery Movement* (Chapel Hill: University of North Carolina Press, 1998).

267 Early women's rights activists such as Susan B. Anthony and Elizabeth Cady Stanton are reasonably well known, but conservative evangelical women have been almost completely neglected. I discuss these some of these women in Mark David Hall, "Beyond Self-Interest: The Political Theory and Practice of Evangelical Women in Antebellum America," *Journal of Church and State*, 44 (Summer 2002): 477–99.

268 Paul J. Polgar, *Standard-Bearers of Equality: America's First Abolitionist Movement* (Chapel Hill: University of North Carolina Press, 2019).

269 The Presbyterian denomination contained a fair number of evangelicals, but it was not as pervasively evangelical as the Methodist and Baptist denominations. It split over slavery in 1838.

270 *Quakers and Abolition*, ed. Brycchan Carey and Geoffrey Gilbert Plank (Urbana: University of Illinois Press, 2018), 4.

271 The Grimké sisters were the subject of Gerda Lerner's landmark work *The Grimké Sisters from South Carolina: Rebels Against Slavery* (Boston: Houghton Mifflin, 1967). A number of Quaker abolitionists drifted from Christian orthodoxy, including the Grimké sisters. See, for instance, Anna M. Speicher, *The Religious World of Antislavery Women: Spirituality in the Lives of Five Abolitionist Lecturers* (Syracuse: Syracuse University Press, 2000) and Mark Perry, *Lift Up Thy Voice: The Grimké Family's Journey From Slaveholders to Civil Rights Leaders* (New York: Penguin Books, 2001).

272 Lerner, *Grimké Sisters*, 227.

273 According to Robert Baird, there were 64,000 Friends and 10,000 Hicksite Friends in 1855. Baird's figures are cited in Smith, *Revivalism and Social Reform*, 21. I divided the total number of Quakers by the 1850 census figures for the total U.S. population to reach their percentage of the population. The 1850 census data is available here: https://www.census.gov/history/www/through_the_decades/fast_facts/1850_fast_facts.html.

274 William Hague, *William Wilberforce: The Life of the Great Anti-Slave Trade Campaigner* (Orlando: Harcourt, 2008).

275 Quoted in Kidd, *God of Liberty*, 157.

276 Polgar, *Standard-Bearers of Equality*.

277 Frances FitzGerald, *The Evangelicals: The Struggle to Shape America* (New York: Simon and Schuster, 2017), 40–43.

278   "Harriet Livermore to James Madison, Oct. 28, 1829," Founders Early Access, https://rotunda.upress.virginia. edu/founders/default.xqy?keys=FOEA-print-02-02-02-1900.

279   Sojourner Truth, *The Narrative of Sojourner Truth* (New York: Oxford University Press, 1991), 164.

280   Truth, *The Narrative of Sojourner Truth*, 164–65.

281   For the original transcript of this speech and commentary on different editions of it, see Jeffrey C. Stewart's introduction to *Narrative of Sojourner Truth* (New York: Oxford University Press, 1991), xxxiii–xxxv, 133–35.

282   Steward, *Holy Warriors*, 140; Kate Clifford Larson, *Bound for the Promised Land: Harriet Tubman, Portrait of an American Hero* (New York: Ballantine Books, 2004), xvii.

283   Kidd, *Who is an Evangelical?*, 49.

284   Stewart, *Holy Warriors*, 52

285   Smith, *Revivalism and Social Reform*, 180.

286   Stewart, *Holy Warriors*, 70; Walters, *American Reformers*, 80–81; Jeffrey, *Great Silent Army*, 86–91.

287   Beecher, *An Essay on Slavery* (Philadelphia, 1837), 13–14, 37, 52, 109. Beecher criticized slavery elsewhere. For instance, in *The Elements of Mental and Moral Philosophy, Founded upon Experience, Reason, and the Bible* (Hartford, 1831), Beecher wrote, "Two millions of slaves, deprived of the best blessing and the dearest rights of humanity, are held in the most degrading bondage, by a nation who yearly and publicly acknowledges their perfect and unalienable rights," 261.

288   Beecher, *An Essay on Slavery*, 19–20.

289   Beecher, *An Essay on Slavery*, 50.

290   Beecher, *An Essay on Slavery*, 127. Angelina Grimké responded to this critique in *Letters to Catherine E. Beecher*, (Boston: 1838).

291   Beecher, *An Essay on Slavery*, 52.

292   Beecher, *An Essay on Slavery*, 52.

293   Kathryn Kish Sklar, *Catharine Beecher: A Study in American Domesticity* (New Haven: Yale University Press, 1973), 59.

294   Robert E. Conrad, *Destruction of Brazilian Slavery, 1850–1888* (Berkeley: University of California Press, 1972), 284.

295   Perry, *Lift Up They Voice*, 177–87.

296   Stewart, *Holy Warriors*, 165.

297   Joan D. Hendrick, *Harriet Beecher Stowe: A Life* (New York: Oxford University Press, 1994), vii.

298   Lucas E. Morel, *Lincoln and the American Founding* (Carbondale: Southern Illinois University Press, 2020).

299   As did the 14th and 15th amendments. But, of course, great injustices remained. *After* the Civil War, the three African American heroes discussed above, Frederick Douglass, Sojourner Truth, and Harriet Tubman, were removed from trains or street cars because of the color of their skin. After Reconstruction, Southern states adopted laws requiring segregation and hindering the ability of African Americans to vote. Larson, *Bound for the Promised Land*, 231–32.

300   Claudio Saunt provides an excellent overview of the removal of all five tribes in *Unworthy Republic: The Dispossession of Native Americans and the Road to Indian Territory* (New York: W.W. Norton, 2020).

301   Steve Inskeep, *Jacksonland: President Andrew Jackson, Cherokee Chief John Ross, and a Great American Land Grab* (New York: Penguin, 2015), 171–180. *The Cherokee Removal: A Brief History with Documents* 2nd (New York: Bedford, 2005) provides an accessible overview of this controversy and selections of the relevant primary source documents.

302 Inskeep, *Jacksonland*, 171–180.

303 Quoted in John West, *The Politics of Reason and Revelation: Religion and Civil Life in the New Nation* (Lawrence: University of Kansas Press, 1996), 182.

304 Quoted in Inskeep, *Jacksonland*, 218.

305 The circular was published in multiple newspapers and edited volumes. I reference the copy published in *The Religious Examiner*, ed. Samuel Findley (Washington, OH: 1829), 3: 67–73. The quotations are from page 70.

306 Beecher, *Circular Letter*, 72. Beecher quoted Esther 4:14, although she reworded it slightly to read "Who knoweth whether thou art come to the kingdom for such a cause as this?" For additional discussion about the circular and the women who signed petitions, see Mary Hersberger, "Mobilizing Women, Anticipating Abolition: The Struggle Against Indian Removal in the 1830s," *Journal of American History* 86 (June, 1999), 15–40 and Alisse Theodore Portnoy, "'Female Petitioners Can Lawfully be Heard': Negotiating Female Decorum, United States Politics, and Political Agency, 1829–1830," *Journal of the Early Republic* 23 (Winter, 2003): 573–610.

307 "Circular" Cherokee Phoenix, https://www.wcu.edu/library/DigitalCollections/CherokeePhoenix/Vol2/no39/circular-page-2-column-3b-page-3-column-2b.html.

308 West, *Politics of Reason and Revelation*, 185–198, 278.

309 Inskeep, *Jacksonland*, 218.

310 Saunt, *Unworthy Republic*, 79.

311 Inskeep, *Jacksonland*, 257.

312 Inskeep, *Jacksonland*, 255–62.

313 Inskeep, *Jacksonland*, 265–336.

314 Inskeep, *Jacksonland*, 300–336.

315   Perdue and Green, *The Cherokee Removal*, 168.

316   Beecher, "Circular Letter," 67.

317   Ronald G. Walters writes about this phenomenon in his fine book *American Reformers*, ix–xi.

318   West, *Politics of Reason and Revelation*, 88–97.

319   Abzug, Robert. *Cosmos Crumbling: American Reform and the Religious Imagination* (New York: Oxford University Press, 1994), 81–104.

320   See Mark David Hall, *Did America Have a Christian Founding?: Separating Modern Myth from Historical Truth* (Nashville: Nelson Books, 2019); Daniel L. Dreisbach and Mark David Hall, ed., *Faith and the Founders of the American Republic* (New York: Oxford University Press, 2014); and Daniel L. Dreisbach, Mark David Hall, and Jeffry H. Morrison, ed., *The Forgotten Founders on Religion and Public Life* (Notre Dame: University of Notre Dame Press, 2009); Daniel L. Dreisbach, Mark David Hall, and Jeffry H. Morrison, ed. *The Founders on God and Government* (Lanham: Rowman and Littlefield, 2004).

321   Daniel L. Dreisbach and Mark David Hall, *The Sacred Rights of Conscience: Selected Readings on Religious Liberty and Church–State Relations in the American Founding* (Indianapolis: Liberty Fund Press, 2009), 98; Maura Jane Farrelly, *Anti-Catholicism in America, 1620-1860* (New York: Cambridge University Press, 2018), 36–133; Michael D. Breidenbach, *Our Dear-Bought Liberty: Catholics and Religious Toleration in Early America* (Cambridge: Harvard University Press, 2021).

322   Roger Finke and Rodney Stark, *The Churching of America, 1776-2005: Winners and Losers in Our Religious Economy,* (New Brunswick: Rutgers University Press, 1992), 55; and Mark A. Noll, *A History of Christianity in the United*

States and Canada (Grand Rapids: Eerdmans, 1992), 361; Farrelly, *Anti-Catholicism in America*, 134–161.

323 Maria Monk, *Awful Disclosures of Maria Monk, or, The Hidden Secrets of a Nun's Life in a Convent Exposed*, rev. ed. (New York, 1836); locations 575, 1597 of ebook.

324 Rebecca Theresa Reed, *Six Months in a Convent* (Boston, 1835); Josephine Bunkley, *The Testimony of an Escaped Novice* (New York: 1855), and Rosemond Culbertson, *Rosamond: or, A Narrative of the Captivity and Sufferings of an American Female under the Popish Priests, in the Island of Cuba* (New York, 1836); Farrelly, *Anti-Catholicism in America*,151–56.

325 Samuel F.B. Morse, *Imminent Dangers to the Free Institutions of the United States Through Foreign Immigration* (1835, reprint; New York: Arno Press, 1969), 8.

326 Morse, *Imminent Dangers*, 28.

327 Morse, *Imminent Dangers*, 28.

328 Henry Ward Beecher, *A Plea for the West* (Cincinnati, 1835); William C. Brownlee, *Popery: An Enemy to civil and Religious Liberty and Dangerous to Our Republic* (New York, 1836); Josiah Strong, *Our Country* (New York, 1885).

329 *Syllabus of Errors*, (1864), as quoted in James McPherson, *Battle Cry of Freedom: The Civil War Era* (New York: Oxford University Press, 1988), 132.

330 Breidenbach, *Our Dear-Bought Liberties*; Philip Hamburger, *Separation of Church and State* (Cambridge: Harvard University Press, 2002), 201–219, 229–34; Steven K. Green, *The Third Disestablishment: Church, State, & American Culture, 1940-1975* (New York: Oxford University Press, 2019), 49–51.

331 Hamburger, *Separation of Church and State*, 216.

332 Quoted in Steven K. Green, *The Second Disestablishment: Church and State in Nineteenth-Century America*, (New York: Oxford University Press, 2010), 262.

333 Hamburger, *Separation of Church and State*, 219; Green, *The Second Disestablishment*, 256–87; David Sehat, *The Myth of American Religious Freedom* (New York: Oxford University Press, 2011), 155–168; Stephen Waldman, *Sacred Liberty: America's Long, Bloody, and Ongoing Struggle for Religious Freedom* (New York: HarperOne, 2019), 69–71.

334 Daniel Walker Howe, *What Hath God Wrought: The Transformation of America, 1815-1848* (New York: Oxford University Press, 2007), 751; Waldman, *Sacred Liberty* 76.

335 Waldman, *Sacred Liberty*, 77; Farrelly, *Anti-Catholicism in America*, 150.

336 Mark S. Massa, *Anti-Catholicism in America: The Last Acceptable Prejudice* (New York: Crossroad Books, 2003), 28.

337 Farrelly, *Anti-Catholicism in America, 1620-1860*, 167.

338 McPherson, *Battle Cry of Freedom*, 138–44, 217–18,

339 Abraham Lincoln, *Selected Speeches and Writings* ed. Don E. Fehrenbacher (New York: Vintage Books, 1989), 105–06.

340 Quoted in Green, *Second Disestablishment*, 292.

341 Quoted in Green, *Second Disestablishment*, 293.

342 Quoted in Hamburger, *Separation of Church and State*, 297–98.

343 Hamburger, *Separation of Church and State*, 297–98.

344 Hamburger, *Separation of Church and State*, 334–359.

345 For details about the cartoon, see https://www.harpweek.com/09cartoon/BrowseByDateCartoon.asp?Month=May&Date=8.

346 Hamburger, *Separation of Church and State*, 338.

347 Amicus Curia brief of the Becket Fund for Religious Liberty in Espinoza v. Montana (2019), 11 available here: https://www.supremecourt.gov/DocketPDF/18/18-1195/116251/20190918150903856_No.%20 18-1195tsacTheBecketFundForRegigiousLiberty.pdf.

348   Hamburger, *Separation of Church and State*, 340.

349   Hamburger, *Separation of Church and State*, 340.

350   *Mitchel v. Helms* 530 US 793 (2000), 828–29.

351   *Zelman v. Simmons-Harris* 536 U.S. 639 (2002), 721.

352   Green, *Third Disestablishment*, 16–57.

353   Hamburger, *Separation of Church and State*, 396–422.

354   Waldman, *Sacred Liberty*, 153.

355   Hamburger, *Wall of Separation*, 415–19, 418.

356   Robert A. Slayton, "When a Catholic Terrified the Heartland," *The New York Times*, December 10, 2011, https://campaignstops.blogs.nytimes.com/2011/12/10/when-a-catholic-terrified-the-heartland/.

357   Quoted in Waldman, *Sacred* Liberty, 157.

358   Massa, *Anti-Catholicism in America*, 59.

359   Paul Blanshard, *American Freedom and Catholic Power*, 2nd ed. (Beacon Hill: Beacon Press, 1958), 27.

360   Blanshard, *American Freedom*, 69.

361   Hamburger, *Separation of Church and State*, 454–463.

362   Hamburger, *Separation of Church and State*, 455.

363   Hamburger, *Separation of Church and State*, 455.

364   Hamburger, *Separation of Church and State*, 422–434.

365   Hamburger, *Separation of Church and State*, 463.

366   Hamburger, *Separation of Church and State*, 451.

367   330 U.S. 1, 23 (1947).

368   Green, *Third Disestablishment*, 128.

369   Quoted in Hamburger, *Separation of Church and State*, 471.

370   333 U.S. 203.

371   Hamburger, *Separation of Church and State*, 477.

372   Green, *Third Disestablishment*, 209.

373   Green, *Third Disestablishment*, 209–10.

374   "Transcript: JFK's Speech on His Religion," NPR, December 5, 2007, https://www.npr.org/templates/story/story.php?storyId=16920600.

375   On Kennedy's enduring popularity, see: Frank Newport, "Americans Say Reagan Is the Greatest U.S. President," Gallup, February 18, 2011, https://news.gallup.com/poll/146183/Americans-Say-Reagan-Greatest-President.aspx.

376   Austin Flannery, ed. *Vatican Council II: The Conciliar and Postconciliar Documents*, rev. ed. (Collegeville: Liturgical Press, 1996); Samuel P. Huntington, *The Third Wave: Democratization in the Late 20th Century* (Norman: University of Oklahoma Press, 1991).

377   Of course, anti-Catholicism did not disappear altogether. See Philip Jenkins, *The New Anti-Catholicism: The Last Acceptable Prejudice* (New York: Oxford University Press, 2003); Massa, *Anti-Catholicism in America.*

378   *Abington School District v. Schempp*, 374 U.S. 203 (1963)

379   Green, *Third Disestablishment*, 265–73.

380   Green's *The Third Disestablishment* is, in my opinion, a logical extension of Hamburger's *Separation of Church and State*. Green criticizes Hamburger's work in several places, e.g. *Second Disestablishment*, 8, and *Third Disestablishment*, 7–9, but collectively, their works highlight the anti-Catholic origins of separationism.

381   James Guth, Lyman Kellstedt, Corwin Smidt, and John Green "Religious Influences in the 2004 Presidential Election," *Presidential Studies Quarterly* 36 (June 2006), 227–28. For percentage of Catholics voting for *Bush v. Kerry*, see https://www.cnn.com/ELECTION/2004/pages/results/states/US/P/00/epolls.0.html

382   Waldman, *Sacred Liberty*, 232.

383   The strategy of appointing justices who would overturn Roe finally succeeded in 2022. See *Dobbs v. Jackson Women's Health Organization* (2022), available at: https://www.supremecourt.gov/opinions/21pdf/19-1392_6j37.pdf.

384   "Evangelicals & Catholics Together: The Christian Mission In The Third Millennium," *First Things,*

May 1994, https://www.firstthings.com/article/1994/05/evangelicals-catholics-together-the-christian-mission-in-the-third-millennium.

385 "Ohio Holocaust and Liberators Memorial," Ohio Statehouse, http://www.ohiostatehouse.org/about/capitol-square/statues-and-monuments/ohio-holocaust-and-liberators-memorial.

386 Dan Barker and Annie Laurie Gaylor, "Improper Religious Iconography in Planned Memorial" (Letter, Columbus, OH, 2013), 1, https://ffrf.org/images/Ohio%20Statehouse%20Holocaust%20Memorial.pdf.

387 Dan Barker and Annie Laurie Gaylor, "Improper Religious Iconography in Planned Memorial" (Letter, Columbus, OH, 2013), 2, https://ffrf.org/images/Ohio%20Statehouse%20Holocaust%20Memorial.pdf.

388 Adele Berlin and Maxine Grossman, ed. *The Oxford Dictionary of the Jewish Religion*, 2nd (New York: Oxford University Press, 2011), n.p. (entry for "Magen David").

389 Elon Gilad, "How Israel Got Its Flag and What It Means," Haaretz, May 11, 2016, https://www.haaretz.com/israel-news/.premium-how-israel-got-its-flag-and-what-it-means-1.5381190; National EMS Organization, https://www.mdais.org/en.

390 330 U.S. 1, 14–15, 33 (1947).

391 *Everson v. Board of Education* 330 U.S. 1, 14–15 (1947).

392 See Mark David Hall, *Did America Have a Christian Founding?: Separating Modern Myth from Historical Truth* (Nashville: Nelson Books, 2019); Daniel L. Dreisbach and Mark David Hall, ed., *Faith and the Founders of the American Republic* (New York: Oxford University Press, 2014); and Daniel L. Dreisbach, Mark David Hall, and Jeffry H. Morrison, ed., *The Forgotten Founders on Religion and Public Life* (Notre Dame: University of Notre Dame Press, 2009); Daniel L. Dreisbach, Mark David Hall, and

Jeffry H. Morrison, ed. *The Founders on God and Government* (Lanham: Rowman and Littlefield, 2004).

393   *Marsh v. Chambers*, 463 U.S. 783 (1983).

394   *Marsh*, 787–88.

395   *Marsh*, 786.

396   *Town of Greece v. Galloway*, 572 U.S. ___ (2014).

397   *Greece v. Galloway*, 572 U.S. ___ 9 (2014) (Kennedy, J. majority opinion).

398   *Greece v. Galloway*, 572 U.S. ___ 9 (2014) (Kagan, J. dissenting).

399   In *Engel v. Vitale*, 370 U.S. 421 (1962), the United States Supreme Court declared teacher-led prayer in public schools to be unconstitutional. As a matter of constitutional interpretation, this decision is erroneous. There are, however, good prudential and theological reasons to not have *teacher-led* prayer in public schools, but students should be free to pray on their own or in voluntary groups.

400   *Lynch v. Donnelly*, 465 U.S. 668, 674 (1984).

401   *County of Allegheny v. ACLU*, 492 U.S. 573 (1989).

402   *Allegheny v. ACLU*, 659.

403   *Allegheny v. ACLU*, 679. In his opinion, Kennedy explained that it is the principles embraced by the founders that are determinative. Therefore, the fact that "displays commemorating religious holidays were not commonplace in 1791" does not entail that such displays are inconsistent with the values underlying the Establishment Clause. *Allegheny v. ACLU*, 669.

404   *Marsh v. Chambers*, 463 U.S. 783, 786 (1983).

405   *American Legion, et al. v. American Humanist Association*, 588 U.S. __, 2–5 (2019) (Alito, J.).

406   Peter Gardella, *American Civil Religion: What Americans Hold Sacred* (New York: Oxford University Press, 2014), 191, 195.

407 Descriptions of all but the last of the crosses mentioned above come from a professors' *amicus* brief (hereinafter "Professors' brief") I helped write for *The American Legion et al. v. American Humanist Association.* The brief is available here: https://www.supremecourt.gov/DocketPDF/17/17-1717/77608/20181226144524325_17-1717%20Professors%20Amicus%20Brief.pdf. The quotations may be found on pages 16–19.

408 *American Legion v. American Humanist Association*, 588 U.S. __ (2019).

409 *American Legion v. American Humanist Association*, (Alito, J.).

410 *American Legion v. American Humanist Association*, 28.

411 *American Legion v. American Humanist Association*, 28.

412 *American Legion v. American Humanist Association*, 1–12 (Ginsburg, J., dissenting).

413 "Jeffersonian Walls and Madisonian Lines: The Supreme Court's Use of History in Religion Clause Cases," *Oregon Law Review* 85 (2006): 563–614.

414 Barry A. Kosmin and Seymour P. Lachman, *One Nation Under God: Religion in Contemporary American Society* (New York: Harmony Books, 1993), 28–29; David G. Dalin, "Jews, Judaism, and the American Founding," in Dreisbach and Hall, *Faith and the Founders of the American Republic*, 63.

415 Frank Newport, "This Christmas, 78% of Americans Identify as Christian," *Gallup*, December 24, 2009, https://news.gallup.com/poll/124793/this-christmas-78-americans-identify-christian.aspx.

416 "Modeling the Future of Religion in America," Pew Research Center, September 13, 2022, https://www.pewresearch.org/religion/2022/09/13/modeling-the-future-of-religion-in-america/.

417 "National Cemetery Administration," U.S. Department of Veterans Affairs, last modified April 17, 2015, https://www.cem.va.gov/cem/history/hmhist.asp.

418 "Emblems of Belief," U.S. Department of Veterans Affairs, last modified November 2, 2021, https://www.cem.va.gov/cem/hmm/emblems.asp. These are not just theoretical possibilities, even for small religious groups. For instance, according to Jay Wexler, there are eight Wiccan pentacle markers in Arlington National Cemetery. Wexler, *Our Non-Christian Nation: How Atheists, Satanists, Pagans, and Others Are Demanding Their Rightful Place in Public Life* (Stanford: Redwood Press, 2019), 56.

419 Paul Finkelman, "The Ten Commandments on the Courthouse Lawn and Elsewhere," *Fordham Law Review* 73 (March 2005): 1477–1520.

420 Declaration of Judge E.J. Ruegemer for *Card v. City of Everett*, No. CV03-2385L, Sept. 19, 2003, 2.

421 Declaration of Judge E.J. Ruegemer, 3.

422 Declaration of Judge E.J. Ruegemer, 3–4. DeMille was only involved in the early stages of what has been referred to as the Eagles' Ten Commandment Project. Sue A. Hoffman provides an extensive history of the origins and history of this project in: *In Search of God and the Ten Commandments: One Person's Journey to Preserve a Small Part of America's God-given Values and Freedoms* (self-published, 2014), 76–79.

423 *Van Orden v. Perry*, (2006), 545 U.S. 677, 681 (2005) (Rehnquist, C.J., majority opinion).

424 *Van Orden v. Perry*, 125 S. Ct. 2854 (2005).

425 *McCreary County v. ACLU of Kentucky*, 125 S. Ct. 2722 (2005).

426 See especially *Van Orden v. Perry*, 545 U.S. 677, 700–705 (2005) (Breyer, J., concurring).

427 *Van Orden v. Perry*, 545 U.S. 677, 688 (2005).

428 *Van Orden v. Perry*, 688–89.

429 *Marsh v. Chambers*, 786.

430 Mark David Hall, Expert Report in *Donna Cave v. John Thurston*, No. 4: 18-cv-00342-KGB and *Anne Orsi v. John Thurston*, No. 4: 18-cv-343-KGB, Nov. 6, 2019, 46–56.

431 John Sharp, "Ten Commandments amendment overwhelmingly approved," AL.com, last modified November 7, 2018, https://www.al.com/politics/2018/11/ten-commandments-amendment-cruising-to-overwhelming-passage.html.

432 Ten Commandments-GA, Inc., "Placing Historical Documents in Georgia's Public Buildings," press release, May 8, 2012, http://tencommandmentsga.org/downloads/PlacingHistoricalDisplays.pdf.

433 Matthew Daigle, "Art, courts, and the legacy of Harry Cochrane," *Sun Journal*, March 10, 2019, https://www.sunjournal.com/2019/03/10/art-courts-and-the-legacy-of-monmouths-harry-cochrane/.

434 "Moral and Divine Law," Minnesota Historical Society, http://www.mnhs.org/capitol/learn/art/8949.

435 "Queens Supreme Court, Jamaica," Forgotten New York, November 13, 2015, https://forgotten-ny.com/2015/11/queens-supreme-court-jamaica/.

436 Anna Marie Jehorek, *The Pennsylvania Capitol*, "Pull Over and Let Me Out," https://pulloverandletmeout.com/touring-the-pennsylvania-state-capitol-in-harrisburg/.

437 Albert M. Tannler, *Architecture Feature: Edward Trumbull in Pittsburgh*, Pittsburgh History & Landmarks Foundation, https://phlf.org/2017/10/02/architecture-feature-edward-trumbull-pittsburgh/.

438 *Marsh v. Chambers*, 463 U.S. 783, 786 (1983).

439 "History & Culture," National Park Service, last modified January 18, 2022, https://www.nps.gov/wamo/learn/historyculture/index.htm.

440 Judith M. Jacob, *The Washington Monument: A Technical History and Catalog of the Commemorative Stones* (Wash-

ington, D.C.: National Park Service, 2005), 1, https://www.
nps.gov/parkhistory/online_books/wamo/stones.pdf.

441 Jacob, *The Washington Monument*, 192.

442 Jacob, *The Washington Monument*, 57.

443 Jacob, *The Washington Monument*, 190.

444 Clint W. Ensign, *Inscriptions of a Nation: Collected Quotations from Washington Monuments* (Washington, D.C. Congressional Quarterly, 1994).

445 Ensign, *Inscriptions*, 22, 24, 31.

446 Ensign, *Inscriptions*, 57, 58; Timm Schmig, *Our Story in Stones* (self-published, 2017), 12–13.

447 36 U.S.C. 302; 31 U.S.C. 5112(d)(1).

448 4 U.S.C. § 4.

449 *Elk Grove Unified School District v. Newdow*, 542 U.S. 1 (2004); Raelian Movement, "Raelian Seeking US Citizenship Sues to Remove 'So Help Me God' from Oath," PR Newswire, May 7, 2018, https://www.prnewswire.com/news-releases/raelian-seeking-us-citizenship-sues-to-remove-so-help-me-godfrom-oath-300642809.html.

450 "Ohio Holocaust and Liberators Memorial," Ohio Statehouse, http://www.ohiostatehouse.org/about/capitol-square/statues-and-monuments/ohio-holocaust-and-liberators-memorial; "About the Memorial," The Ohio Holocaust and Liberators Memorial, https://ohioholocaustmemorial.org/.

451 "Ohio Holocaust and Liberators Memorial," Ohio Statehouse, http://www.ohiostatehouse.org/about/capitol-square/statues-and-monuments/ohio-holocaust-and-liberators-memorial.

452 "South Carolina Holocaust," One Columbia, https://www.onecolumbiasc.com/public-art/south-carolina-holocaust-memorial/; "New Orleans Holocaust Memorial," *Star of David* (blog), May 6, 2007, http://star-of-david.blogspot.com/2007/05/new-orleans-holocaust-memorial.html. Stars of David, alongside other

religious symbols, are included in the National September 11 Memorial & Museum: https://www.911memorial.org/blog/collection-symbols-forged-wtc-steel.

453 *American Legion v. American Humanist Association*, 588 U.S. __, 30 (2019) (Alito, J.). See also: Nathan Rapoport, "Monument to Six Million Jewish Martyrs," Association for Public Art, https://www.associationforpublicart.org/artwork/monument-to-six-million-jewish-martyrs/.

454 Samuel Gruber, "USA: Charleston's Holocaust Memorial in Shadow of Calhoun Monument," *Samuel Gruber's Jewish Art & Monuments* (blog), February 26, 2017, http://samgrubersjewishartmonuments.blogspot.com/2017/02/usa-charlestons-holocaust-memorial-in.html; "Charleston Holocaust Memorial, Charleston South Carolina," Waymarking.com, August 27, 2008, http://www.waymarking.com/waymarks/WM4HN4_Charleston_Holocaust_Memorial_Charleston_South_Carolina.

455 Avril Alba, *The Holocaust Memorial Museum Sacred Secular Space* (London: Palgrave Macmillan, 2015), 78–79, 66; "Frequently Asked Research Questions," United States Holocaust Memorial Museum, accessed November 2, 2022, https://www.ushmm.org/collections/ask-a-research-question/frequently-asked-questions#1; and Ryan Coonerty, *Etched in Stone: Enduring Words From Our Nation's Monuments* (Washington, D.C.: National Geographic, 2008), 112.

456 The Memorial's website describes Confucius as "a Chinese teacher, philosopher and political figure," but some followers and scholars consider him to be a religious figure as well. On this debate, see: Peter L. Berger, "Is Confucianism a Religion?" *The American Interest*, February 15, 2012, https://www.the-american-interest.com/2012/02/15/is-confucianism-a-religion/.

457 The memorial was built by the Wassmuth Center for Human Rights on land owned by the City of Boise. It is considered to be a public park. At one point, all of the above mentioned quotations were listed on this website: https://annefrankmemorial.org/memorial-tour/#-section9 (accessed July 10, 2019). This page is now inactive, but I had the opportunity to visit the memorial and verify the quotations in the summer of 2020.

458 "Srila Prabhupada's Hare Krishna Tree," http://www.harekrsna.com/philosophy/acarya/newyork.htm.

459 *American Legion v. American Humanist Association*, 588 U.S. __, 30 (2019) (Alito, J.). As well, the Memorial's "design incorporates water for sacred ceremonies, benches for gathering and reflection, and four lances where veterans, family members, tribal leaders, and others can tie cloths for prayers and healing." See: "National Native American Veterans Memorial," National Museum of the American Indian, https://americanindian.si.edu/nnavm/.

460 American governments (national, state, and municipal) have long recognized Christian holidays (especially Christmas), but only in recent decades have they begun to recognize non-Christian ones as well (https://washington.org/visit-dc/holidays-white-house-first-family-traditions). Since the turn of this century, for instance, the White House has hosted events to commemorate Hindu, Islamic, Jewish, and Sikh holy days (https://s3.amazonaws.com/becketpdf/Van-Orden-USSC-BFRL-Amicus.pdf, esp. 6–7).

461 See, for instance, Justice Breyer's suggestion in the Bladensburg cross case oral arguments that: "History counts. And so, yes, okay, but no more." Available at: https://www.supremecourt.gov/oral_arguments/ar-

gument_transcripts/2018/17-1717_7l48.pdf, 61; and his concurring opinion in *American Legion et al. v. American Humanist Association*, 588 U.S. __, 2 (2019). See: Garrett Epps, "Religious Monuments Are Fine Now—If They're Old: The Supreme Court's Peace Cross decision is very messy," *The Atlantic*, June 21, 2019, https://www.theatlantic.com/ideas/archive/2019/06/peace-cross-splits-supreme-court/592222/.

462   *Marsh v. Chambers*, 463 U.S. 783, 786 (1983).

463   For an excellent, balanced overview of this tradition see Richard Bushman, *Mormonism: A Very Short Introduction* (New York: Oxford University Press, 2008).

464   Bushman, *Mormonism*, 86–88.

465   *Reynolds v. United States*, 98 U.S. 145 (1879).

466   "Official Declaration 1," The Church of Jesus Christ of Latter-Day Saints, https://www.lds.org/scriptures/dc-testament/od/1.

467   *Brown v. Burham*, No. 14-4117 (10th Cir. 2016), 4 and *passim*.

468   Steven K. Green's *The Second Disestablishment: Church and State in Nineteenth-Century America*, (New York: Oxford University Press, 2010) and David Sehat's *The Myth of American Religious Freedom* (New York: Oxford University Press, 2011) document the many ways in which states often did not protect the religious liberty of minorities.

469   *Cantwell v. Connecticut*, 310 US 296 (1940).

470   This movement started earlier, but it accelerated as America approached the Second World War. For an excellent overview, see Richard J. Ellis, *To the Flag: The Unlikely History of the Pledge of Allegiance* (Lawrence: University Press of Kansas, 2005).

471   *Minersville School District v. Gobitis*, 310 U.S. 586 (1940).

472   *West Virginia State Board of Education v. Barnette*, 319 U.S. 624, 638 (1943).

473   *West Virginia State Board of Education v. Barnette*, 642.

474   *Sherbert v. Verner*, 374 U.S. 398 (1963).

475   *Wisconsin v. Yoder*, 406 US 205 (1972).

476   See, for instance, *Zelman v. Simmons-Harris*, 536 U.S. 639 (2002), which upheld Ohio's school voucher program.

477   *Employment Division v. Smith*, 494 U.S. 872 (1990)

478   31 Fed. Reg. 4679 (1966); 21 C.F.R. § 1307.31

479   Hall, "Religious Accommodations and the Common Good."

480   Marci A. Hamilton, *God vs. the Gavel: Religion and the Rule of Law*, 2nd rev. ed. (New York: Cambridge University Press, 2015); Alan Rogers, *The Child Cases: How America's Religious Exemption Laws Harm Children* (Amherst: University of Massachusetts Press, 2014).

481   Seth M. Asser and Rita Swan, "Child Fatalities From Religion-Motivated Medical Neglect," Pediatrics 101 (1998), 625–629. See also Rita Swan, "Faith-Based Medical Neglect: for Providers and Policymakers," *Journal of Child & Adolescent Trauma* 13 (2020), 343–353.

482   Brian Tashman, "Robert George Warns of Obama's 'Massive Assault on Religious Liberty,'" *People for the American Way*, Right Wing Watch, February 15, 2012, http://www.rightwingwatch.org/content/robert-george-warns-obamas-massive-assault-religious-liberty.

483   David French, "Yes, American Religious Liberty Is in Peril," *Wall Street Journal*, July 26, 2019, https://www.wsj.com/articles/yes-american-religious-liberty-is-in-peril-11564152873.

484   American Civil Liberties Union, "Using Religion to Discriminate," ACLU, https://www.aclu.org/feature/using-religion-discriminate; Americans United for Separation of Church and State, Protect Thy Neighbor, "Protecting Our Neighbors," http://www.protectthyneighbor.org/.

485 *Hosanna-Tabor Evangelical Lutheran Church & School v. Equal Employment Opportunity Commission*, 565 US 171, 196 (2012).

486 *Burwell v. Hobby Lobby Stores*, 573 U.S. 682 (2014); *Hosanna-Tabor Evangelical Lutheran Church & School v. Equal Employment Opportunity Commission*, 565 US 171 (2012).

487 U.S. Commission on Civil Rights, "Peaceful Coexistence: Reconciling Nondiscrimination Principles with Civil Liberties," (briefing report, Washington, DC, 2016), 20, https://www.usccr.gov/pubs/Peaceful-Coexistence-09-07-16.PDF.

488 See, for instance, *Elane Photography, L.L.C v. Willock*, 2013-NMSC-040, 309 P.3d 53 (concerning a photographer in New Mexico); *In the Matter of Melissa Elaine Klein, Interim Order, Commissioner of the Bureau of Labor and Industries*, Case Nos. 44-14 and 45-14, January 29, 2015 (concerning bakers in Oregon); and *State of Washington v. Arlene's Flowers*, No. 13-2-008715, February 18, 2015 (concerning a florist in Washington State).

489 A principle reiterated by the Court in *Sharonell Fulton, et al., v. City of Philadelphia*, 593 U.S. ___ (2021).

490 584 U.S. ___ (2018), 13–14.

491 584 U.S. ___ (2018), 13–14.

492 *Melissa Buck v. Robert Gordon*, 429 F. Supp. 3d 447, 451 (W.D. Mich. 2019), https://s3.amazonaws.com/becket-newsite/Buck-v.-Gordon.pdf.

493 Jeffrey Cook, "Beto O'Rourke said he would revoke tax-exempt status from religious organizations that oppose same-sex marriage," *ABC News*, October 11, 2019, https://abcnews.go.com/Politics/beto-orourke-revoke-tax-exempt-status-religious-organizations/story?id=66213718.

494 Justice Samuel Alito, dissenting in *Calvary Chapel Dayton Valley v. Sisolak*, 591 US ___ (2020) available at: https://

www.supremecourt.gov/opinions/19pdf/19a1070_08li.pdf.

495   Hamilton, *God vs. the Gavel*; Brian Leiter, *Why Tolerate Religion?* (Princeton: Princeton University Press, 2013); John Corvino, Ryan T. Anderson, and Sherif Girgis, *Debating Religious Liberty and Discrimination* (New York: Oxford University Press, 2017) (Corvino's chapters); Richard Schragger and Micah Schwarzman, "Against Religious Institutionalism," *Virginia Law Review* 99 (2013), 917–985.

496   Micah Schwartzman, "What if Religion Is Not Special?," *University of Chicago Law Review* 79 (2012), 1350–1427.

497   Brian Leiter, *Why Tolerate Religion?* (Princeton: Princeton University Press, 2013).

498   In *United States v. Seeger*, 380 US 163 (1965) and *Welsh v. United States*, 398 US 333 (1970) the United States Supreme Court engaged in creative statutory interpretation to protect pacifists who were not religious (at least in a traditional sense), but to this day, the United States Code protects only religious pacifists, 50 U.S.C. § 3806(j). I believe non-religious pacifists who have conscientious objections to war should be protected, but it is telling that Congress has only chosen to protect those who are pacifists for religious reasons. For discussion of a wide range of religious accommodations, see my essay "Religious Accommodations and the Common Good" available at: https://www.heritage.org/civil-society/report/religious-accommodations-and-the-common-good.

499   Christopher C. Lund "Religion Is Special Enough." *Virginia Law Review* 103 (2017), 481–524, 486. See also Owen Anderson, "The First Amendment and Natural Religion," Janice Tzuling Chik, "The Philosophical Meaning of Religious Exercise," and John Finnis,

"Freedom of Religion: Special, Valuable, and Qualified," in *The Cambridge Companion to The First Amendment and Religious Liberty,* ed. Michael D. Breidenbach and Owen Anderson (New York: Cambridge University Press, 2020), 15–97.

500 "Ten Reasons We Need Rigorous Research on Effective Compassion," *University of St. Thomas's Law Journal* symposium 15 (Spring 2019), 662. Johnson's article is one of ten essays in a symposium entitled "Religious Freedom and the Common Good." Collectively, they make a strong case that religion promotes the common good.

501 Mark David Hall, "America's Founders, Religious Liberty, and the Common Good," *University of St. Thomas's Law Journal* 15 (Spring 2019), 642–661; Nilay Saiya and Stuti Manchanda, "Paradoxes of Pluralism, Privilege, and Persecution: Explaining Christian Growth and Decline Worldwide," *Sociology of Religion* 20 (2021), 1–19.

502 Douglas NeJaime and Reva B. Siegel, "Religious Accommodation, and Its Limits, in a Pluralistic Society," in *Religious Freedom, LGBT Rights, and the Prospects for Common Ground* ed. William N. Eskridge, Jr. and Robin Fretwell Wilson (New York: Cambridge University Press, 2019), 71.

503 NeJaime and Siegel are concerned about harms other than dignitary harms, such as harms that might come about because of medical conscience protections. NeJaime and Siegel, Religious Accommodations," but see Robin Fretwell Wilson, "Matters of Conscience: Lessons for Same-Sex Marriage from the Healthcare Context," in *Same-Sex Marriage and Religious Liberty: Emerging Conflicts* ed. Douglas Laycock, Anthony R. Picarello, Jr., and Robin Fretwell Wilson (Lanham:

Rowman & Littlefield, 2008), 77–102 and Luke Goodrich, "The Health Care and Conscience Debate" *Engage* 12 (June 2011), 121–27.

504 *Texas v. Johnson*, 491 US 397 (1989); Snyder v. Phelps, 562 US 443 (2011).

505 Governments have a compelling interest in preventing some denials of service, even if for religious reasons. For instance, the Supreme Court properly held that a business owner could not refuse to serve African Americans because of his religious convictions. See *Newman v. Piggie Park Enterprises, Inc.*, 390 U.S. 400 (1968). For an excellent argument supporting this result, see John D. Inazu, *Confident Pluralism: Surviving and Thriving through Deep Difference* (Chicago: University of Chicago Press, 2016).

506 Douglas Ernst, "Christian activists booted from Seattle coffee shop," *The Washington Times*, October 6, 2017, https://www.washingtontimes.com/news/2017/oct/6/christian-activists-booted-from-seattle-coffee-sho/.

507 For an image of the bust, see: https://npg.si.edu/object/npg_NPG.72.70. Sanger's name is being removed from some locations. See: Carrie Mumah, "Planned Parenthood of Greater New York Announces Intent to Remove Margaret Sanger's Name from NYC Health Center," Planned Parenthood of Greater New York, July 21, 2020, https://www.plannedparenthood.org/planned-parenthood-greater-new-york/about/news/planned-parenthood-of-greater-new-york-announces-intent-to-remove-margaret-sangers-name-from-nyc-health-center.

508 Zoë Robinson, "Constitutional Personhood," *George Washington Law Review* 84 (June 2016), 646.

509 Steven D. Smith, "Corporate Religious Liberty and the Culture Wars," Breidenbach and Anderson, *Cambridge Companion*, 342.

510   *Santa Clara v. Southern Pacific Railroad*, 118 US 394 (1886).

511   *The New York Times Company v. Sullivan*, 376 US 254 (1964).

512   See, for example, *Order of St. Benedict v. Steinhauser*, 234 US 640 (1914) and *Presbyterian Church in the United States v. Mary Elizabeth Blue Hull Memorial Presbyterian Church*, 393 US 440 (1969)

513   Zoë Robinson, "The First Amendment Religion Clauses in the United States Supreme Court," in Breidenbach and Anderson, *Cambridge Companion*, 245.

514   *Hosanna-Tabor Evangelical Lutheran Church & School v. Equal Employment Opportunity Commission*, 565 US 171, 196 (2012); *Our Lady of Guadalupe School v. Morrisey-Berru*, 591 U.S. ___ (2020)

515   Steven D. Smith, "Corporate Religious Liberty and the Culture Wars," Breidenbach and Anderson, *Cambridge Companion*, 340.

516   Personal correspondence, Steven D. Smith to Mark David Hall, May 1, 2020.

517   *Burwell v. Hobby Lobby Stores*, 134 S.Ct. 2751 (2014).

518   *Gallagher v. Crown Kosher Super Market, Inc.*, 366 US 617 (1961).

519   *McGowan v. Maryland*, 366 U.S. 420 (1961); *Two Guys v. McGinley*, 366 U.S. 582 (1961); *Braunfeld v. Brown*, 366 U.S. 599 (1961); *Gallagher v. Crown Kosher Market* (1961).

520   Hannah Dineen, "Blue Laws Prohibit Many Stores from Being open on Thanksgiving," News Center Maine, November 25, 2019, https://www.newscentermaine.com/article/life/blue-laws-prevent-many-stores-from-being-open-on-thanksgiving-day/97-67d216e0-70bc-415f-88d1-4fd8378e1cf4#:~:text=In%20Maine%2C%20blue%20

laws%2oprohibit,%3A%2oChristmas%2C%2oEaster%2oand%2oThanksgiving.

521 "8 States with the Strangest Alcohol Laws." Serving Alcohol Inc., https://servingalcohol.com/8-states-with-the-strangest-alcohol-laws/#:~:text=Stop%2o in%2othe%2oname%2oof,a%2obrewery%2oor%2o a%2owinery.

522 Zoë Robinson, "Constitutional Personhood," *George Washington Law Review* 84 (June 2016), 646; Christopher Caldwell, *The Age of Entitlement: America Since the Sixties* (New York: Simon & Schuster, 2020); Andrew R. Lewis, *The Rights Turn in Conservative Christian Politics: How Abortion Transformed the Culture Wars* (New York: Cambridge University Press, 2017).

523 Robinson, "Constitutional Personhood," 646.

524 Of course, the First Amendment only restricted the national government until it was applied to the states through the Fourteenth Amendment. But many founders helped craft bills of rights or laws intended to protect rights in their states.

525 Dalia Fahmy, "7 facts about Southern Baptists," Pew Research Center, June 7, 2019, https://www.pewresearch. org/fact-tank/2019/06/07/7-facts-about-southern-baptists/#:~:text=1The%2oSouthern%2oBaptist%2o Convention,Center's%202014%2oReligious%2oLandscape%2oStudy.

526 Quinnipiac University. July 23-28, 2015. N=1,644 registered voters nationwide. Margin of error ± 2.4. "LGBT p. 2," Pollingreport.com, https://www.pollingreport. com/lgbt2.htm.

527 Personal conversation with Austin Nimocks, the lead attorney defending Stutzman who asked me to be an expert witness in the case (November 3, 2014).

528　Josh Friedes, as quoted in Lornet Turnbull, "State's case against florist fires up gay-marriage critics," *Seattle Times*, April 17, 2013, http://seattletimes.com/html/localnews/2020803087_weddingflowersxml.html.

529　There are, of course, wedding vender providers in other states who have such convictions, but given the number of cases that have arisen, there appear to be quite few of them. This makes a great deal of sense as business owners have profound incentives to serve, not turn away, customers.

530　Christopher C. Lund, "RFRA, State RFRAs, and Religious Minorities, 53 *San Diego Law Review* 163 (2016), 163–184.

531　"About the Center," Christian Legal Society Center for Law and Religious Freedom, https://www.clsreligiousfreedom.org/about-center.

532　There are other religious liberty advocacy groups; I discuss the ones with which I have personally worked. Daniel Bennett provides an excellent overview of these groups in *Defending Faith: The Politics of the Christian Conservative Legal Movement* (Lawrence: University Press of Kansas, 2017). He considers seven such groups, not including Becket, and found that only one of them, The Thomas More Law Center, limits its religious liberty advocacy to Christians (55).

533　Andrew Seidel argues against the last point in *American Crusade: How the Supreme Court is Weaponizing Religious Freedom* (New York: Union Square & Co., 2022). I explain why he is wrong in my review of his book, available here: https://lawliberty.org/book-review/a-crusader-court/.

534　See, for instance, Frederick Mark Gedicks and Rebecca G. Van Tassell, "RFRA Exceptions from the Contraception Mandate: An Unconstitutional Accommodation of Religion," *Harvard Civil Rights–Civil Liberties*

Law Review, Vol. 49, Issue 2 (Summer 2014), 343–384.

535 Michael McConnell, "Establishment and Disestablishment at the Founding, Part I: Establishment of Religion," *William and Mary Law Review* 44 (April 2003), 2131.

536 *Abington v. Schempp*, 374 US 203, 294–96.

537 *Abington v. Schempp*, 298.

538 *Arver v. United States*, 245 US 366 (1918).

539 *Arver v. United States*, 389–390.

540 31 Fed. Reg. 4679 (1966); 21 C.F.R. § 1307.31

541 Quoted in Robert Miller and Ronald Flowers, *Toward Benevolent Neutrality: Church, State, and the Supreme Court* 5th (Waco: Baylor University Press, 1996) 2: 644.

542 Carl H. Esbeck, "Third-Party Burdens, Congressional Accommodations for Religion, and the Establishment Clause," testimony before the Subcommittee on the Constitution and Civil Justice, Committee on the Judiciary, U.S. House of Representatives, February 13, 2015. See also Douglass Laycock, "The Religious Exemption Debate," *Rutgers Journal of Law & Religion* 11 (Fall 2009), 152–154.

543 *Estate of Thornton v. Caldor, Inc.*, 472 U.S. 703, 706 (1985).

544 *Estate of Thornton*, 709.

545 *Cutter v. Wilkinson*, 544 US 709 (2005).

546 Quoted in Mark David Hall, *Roger Sherman and the Creation of the American Republic* (New York: Oxford University Press, 2013), 139

547 Hall, *Roger Sherman*, 145.

548 Mark David Hall, "Religious Accommodations and the Common Good," The Heritage Foundation, October 26, 2015, https://www.heritage.org/civil-society/report/religious-accommodations-and-the-common-good#.

549 Dreisbach and Hall, *Sacred Rights*, 464.

550 Dreisbach and Hall, *Sacred Rights*, 595

551   *Roe v. Wade*, 410 US 113; *Planned Parenthood v. Casey*, 505 US 833. For the estimated number of abortions since Roe, see: Randall O'Bannon Ph.D., "62,502,904 Babies Have Been Killed in Abortions Since Roe v. Wade in 1973," LifeNews.com, January 18, 2021, https://www.lifenews.com/2021/01/18/62502904-babies-have-been-killed-in-abortions-since-roe-v-wade-in-1973/.

552   *Dobbs v. Jackson Women's Health Organization*, 597 U.S. __ (2022).

553   I write "most abortions" because almost every pro-life advocate believes abortions are permissible in a few rare instances, such as when they are necessary to save the life of the mother. On ways pro-life Americans assist women with unwanted pregnancies (and suggesting additional things that might be done), see: Will Sorrell, "What Does a Pro-Life Economy Look Like? Abortion has been a national institution for nearly 50 years. Where should Christians spend their pro-life dollars now?" *Christianity Today*, June 24, 2022, https://www.christianitytoday.com/ct/2022/june-web-only/roe-reversal-dobbs-abortion-pro-life-dollars-economy.html.

554   Thomas Farr, *World of Faith and Freedom: Why International Religious Liberty is Vital to American National Security* (New York: Oxford University Press, 2008), Nina Shea, *In the Lion's Den: A Shocking Account of Persecuted and Martyrdom of Christians Today and How We Should* (Nashville: B&H Publishing, 1997); Paul Marshall and Lela Gilbert, *Their Blood Cries Out* (Dallas: Word Publishing, 1997); "H.R.2431 - International Religious Freedom Act of 1998," Congress.gov, https://www.congress.gov/bill/105th-congress/house-bill/2431.

555   Ryan Anderson, *When Harry Became Sally: Responding to the Transgender Moment* (New York: Encounter

Books, 2018); Ryan Anderson, "When Amazon Erased my Book," *First Things*, February 23, 2021, https://www.firstthings.com/web-exclusives/2021/02/when-amazon-erased-my-book.

ACKNOWLEDGMENTS

This book is dedicated to the five religious liberty advocacy groups with whom I have collaborated in some capacity. There are other such groups, and they are also worthy of our praise and support.

I am profoundly grateful to the editors at Fidelis Books and Post Hill Press, especially Alex Novak and Heather King. The book is far better because of their hard work. The Mercatus Center's Garrett Brown was kind enough to put me in touch with Alex.

During the 2022-2023 academic year, I had the privilege of serving as the Garwood Visiting Fellow in Princeton University's James Madison Program and as a Visiting Scholar at George Mason University's Mercatus Center. I am indebted to both organizations, and to Robby George, Brad Wilson, Matt Franck, Shilo Brooks, Allen Guelzo, Debby Parker, Ben Klutsey, Martha Anderson, and many others for their support and encouragement.

Trey Dimsdale, Jordan Ballor, and Jillian Barr of the Center for Religion, Culture, and Democracy, an initiative of First Liberty Institute, have provided multiple opportunities for me to share my work. I am honored to serve as a Senior Fellow in their fine organization. I am grateful as well to Rob Wonderling and Peter Edman of the Faith and Liberty Discovery Center, and to Alan Crippen, its former director. I've enjoyed working with them on several projects and appreciate their support of my work. If you haven't visited the Center's immersive museum, located on Philadelphia's Independence Mall, make it a priority to do so!

I am thankful for the opportunity to publish portions of this book and my next book with Liberty University's Standing for Freedom Center and Colorado Christian University's Centennial Institute. Many thanks to Ryan Helfenbein, Jeff Hunt, John Wesley Reid, Tom Copeland, and other friends at both institutions.

Over the years, I've had the opportunity to help facilitate programs for the Bill of Rights Institute. I was pleased this year to finally get to meet the Institute's Senior Teaching Fellow Tony Williams. Since 2021, I've also had the privilege of working with Kevin Hoeft, John Duebel, and a host of great colleagues on Florida's Civics Initiative. The Bill of Rights Institute and the Florida Department of Education deserve high praise for their commitment to civics education.

I have taught at George Fox University since 2001 and plan to continue teaching as long as possible. I appreciate the excellent students and colleagues who make it such a wonderful place. Since 2015, I have particular enjoyed facilitating sections of our honors program, one of the best great books programs in the nation. If you are a high school student who loves great books (or parent of such a student), please send me an email or give me a call—I would love to discuss the program with you.

George Fox University has proven to be a great place to balance teaching and scholarship. I am grateful for the leadership of President Robin Baker, Provost Andrea Scott, Executive Dean Joseph Clair, and Department Chair Caitlin Corning. The university provided a much-needed leave of absence that enabled me to complete this book and begin a new one.

Daniel L. Dreisbach, Professor of Justice, Law, and Criminology at American University, has been my friend and collaborator for more than thirty years. We have edited five books together, and have often discussed the problems addressed in this book. He has read much of this manuscript, and it far richer because of his comments.

Most of all, I am grateful for my wonderful wife, Miriam, and children: Joshua, Lydia, and Anna.

ABOUT THE AUTHOR

Author photo by: Chris Low

Mark David Hall is Herbert Hoover Distinguished Professor of Politics and Faculty Fellow in the Honors Program at George Fox University. He is also Associated Faculty at the Center for the Study of Law and Religion at Emory University and a Senior Fellow at

Baylor University's Institute for Studies of Religion. In 2022–2023, he is a Visiting Fellow at Princeton University's James Madison Program and a Visiting Scholar at the Mercatus Center. Mark is also a Senior Fellow with the Center for Religion, Culture & Democracy, an initiative of First Liberty Institute.

Mark earned a BA in political science from Wheaton College (IL) and a PhD in Government from the University of Virginia. He has written, edited, or coedited a dozen books, including *Did America Have a Christian Founding?: Separating Modern Myth from Historical Truth* (Nelson Books, 2019); *Great Christian Jurists in American History* (Cambridge University Press, 2019); *Faith and the Founders of the American Republic* (Oxford University Press, 2014); *Roger Sherman and the Creation of the American Republic* (Oxford University Press, 2012); and *The Forgotten Founders on Religion and Public Life* (University of Notre Dame Press, 2009).